LAURA PAZ

Into the Waiting

A Journey in Wonder and Trust

First edition

ISBN: 979-8-9951846-1-4

Editing by Drew Robinson-Tilton
Proofreading by James Bryant
Proofreading by Audrey Bryant
Proofreading by Mandi Kanei
Cover art by Joshua Bowles

This book was professionally typeset on Reedsy.
Find out more at reedsy.com

Dedicated to God, whose creation teaches me to wonder—mountains that steady me, trees that shelter me, sunsets that show His nearness.

To my husband, who nudges me toward the unknown—reminding me to walk in my dreams, not just think of them.

To my parents, who taught me to think, wonder, and believe.

To my sister, whose encouragement serves as an anchor for my life.

To all of my family, who taught me true service to others.

To my sons—may you grow in wonder and wait on the Lord in joy.

Contents

Introduction

Patience is a virtue. That's what they say anyway. Try telling that to the driver who barreled past me, flipping me off as I slowed to let a pedestrian cross. Here's the thing about patience. In today's world, if you enter a fast food line, from start to finish, you can expect to wait six minutes and 13 seconds on average compared to the possible hours it could take for a home cooked meal. Or consider the instant gratification of immediately finding the answer on my phone when I have some obscure question about the year that the fast food restaurant opened or what it takes to open my own fast food restaurant. Not that all of this is bad, mind you, but you can't say that our greatest skill is waiting.

According to Dr. Seuss in *Oh, the Places You'll Go*,

> *"You can get so confused that you'll start into race down long wiggled roads at a break-necking pace and grind on for miles across weirdish wild space, headed, I fear, toward a most useless place. The waiting place..."*[1]

As brilliant as the man is, he views waiting like the world does, as a "useless place". This isn't how God and His followers, however, should view waiting.

---

[1] Seuss, Dr. Oh, the Places You'll Go! Random House, 1990.

We wait for things all throughout our lives. We wait for our significant other to cross our path, we wait for that job promotion, we wait for that ride at Disneyland. But waiting isn't just about jobs or roller coasters—it is an act of wonder and trust in God.

There are things that we must wait for and wait through. Waiting can be a great teacher. It builds our character, brings us closer to God and much more—but waiting is difficult. For some it's the most trying time of our lives. One of the hardest seasons of waiting for me personally that I've ever experienced was during my pregnancy. For those of you who have experienced it, you know that time warps in the strangest of ways. It flies by, it slows down, and then you are holding on for the biggest change in your life and you don't know when it will actually come.

There was a time in my life when I didn't know if I even wanted children. Growing up it was a scary thing to think about. I was 32 when I finally got married, waiting for the right person to come along (that's a whole other story). About a year after I got married, I found out I was pregnant. I was fine with it, but I didn't feel any strong emotions at the time. But then nine weeks into the pregnancy, I started bleeding. It's common to lose a baby this early. Some don't even know, they just think it's their period. But I knew. I can recall sitting on the floor of my shower, sobbing and bleeding.

I had no way of knowing that it would hit me that hard. I didn't even know if I wanted children but my emotional reaction told me the answer. Then after that, I found myself waiting. Waiting for the child that I now knew I wanted. Measureless moments trickled by before I found out I was pregnant again and then I found myself waiting again for his actual birth. In those moments, I found a statement of faith that I began to live by; "wait on the Lord".

All of what I had experienced came from God's timing. When I was married, pregnant, and when the baby would come. It would be totally up to Him. And oh, was it hard! When I became 39 weeks, the scheduling pressure from the doctors began. Every week they would push me to schedule an induction, every week they would remind me of the risks and the medical data, but I felt the word strongly from God. Wait on the Lord. It's His timing. He knows. And He did know. My son Charlie was born at 42 weeks and 2 days, Valentine's day. He was perfect, healthy. And then, when I became pregnant again, I found myself waiting all over again—for my son Theodore.

Through all this waiting, I leaned on what God whispered to my spirit and confirmed through His Word. This book is for anyone who finds themselves waiting—for healing, for direction, for hope. You will find stories from scripture on how to wait, what to do while waiting, and how others waited. In addition, after each chapter I created an opportunity for a study group with discussions or individual reflection. There is an incredible wonder in waiting for God, but it also requires an immense amount of trust. Let's wade into that waiting together.

* * *

Regardless of the type of waiting you find yourself in, know that I'm praying on your behalf now. I believe that God has heard your prayers and that He will surely answer you. I pray that during this season, the Lord speaks to you in incredible new ways, and I hope these stories help you find strength and peace in your own waiting.

Chapter 1

The Adventure of Waiting

My 19-month-old son has very little concept of time. One toy lasts thirty seconds, maybe a minute—two if I'm lucky. What amazes me are those things that can pull his interest for long periods of time.

As a parent there are always those moments where you have to wait. How do you explain waiting to a baby who can run at lightning speed, yet can't fully express his needs? There was one such day. The invisible timer was ticking down. The peace wouldn't last much longer. I could already sense it—the restless hands and feet. I brace myself for the wiggle and whine before the breakdown.

But then he sees it, right at his eye level. Something I never would have seen. It's a Praying Mantis. To him it's just a giant green bug. It's head turns slowly to look at my son. Each of its legs takes its time to move forward.

So there we are—my son is transfixed. He doesn't even reach to touch it. He just stares, time slowing down—taking in the wonder of this very strange creature that most would walk past.

We stay there longer than I planned, both of us caught in the stillness. And in that moment, I realize—that mundane waiting became an adventure to my son. It's a moment of adventure that, as adults, we often miss. Somewhere along the way we traded curiosity for productivity—thinking the constant doing would get us somewhere.

I step in line for my coffee and I pull out my phone. I sit in the waiting room at the doctor's office checking my texts. I wait for my husband to come home from work—scroll. Those moments of wonder in waiting are lost.

There is only one way for its return, and that's to pull myself back into the moment. Taking back the adventure in life, not just the big but also the small. That same childlike wonder my son had isn't limited to childhood—it's something scholars and scientists chase in their own ways.

Author L. Costa and Bena Kallick call this kind of response one of the Habits of Mind[2]—the intellectual behaviors we employ when confronted with a problem for which we don't immediately have an answer. These can include qualities such as persisting, applying past information to a new situation, thinking about our thinking, etc. One of these Habits of Mind is called "Responding with Wonderment and Awe."

When you are confronted with a problem, a situation you have no explanation for, or what you can't solve in your earthly wisdom, do you respond to it with a sense of awe and wonder? Do you pause in the wake of the mysterious? Or do you sit in frustration?

Take the thing that covers 70% of our planet—the ocean, spanning 360 million square kilometers. Yet, explorers have

---

[2] Costa, Arthur L, and Bena Kallick. *Habits of Mind across the Curriculum.* 2009,

seen less than 0.001% of the deep ocean seafloor[3]. There are millions and millions of kilometers to explore. Scientists claim there are 700,000 to 1 million species of creatures in the ocean, and probably only one-third of them have been discovered. Or take our galaxy—containing 100 billion to 400 billion stars and 100,000 light years across[4]. Yet, here we are a tiny blip in the cosmos. It really puts things into perspective and yet scientists still pour their hearts and souls into discovering more, learning more, and engaging with depths of the ocean and the far reaches of space. From the backyard to the farthest galaxies, the invitation is the same: pause and marvel. There are times when I believe that God created the universe in such a way that teaches us to pause, wonder, and seek. Every wave leading us to the vast ocean. The clouds pushing our thoughts into the great beyond. Every creation—not a wall keeping us from knowing but an invitation for us to keep seeking.

Take one of the most complex theological concepts—the Trinity. Throughout scripture God presents Himself as one in three different persons. As readers of the Word, we take time to engage with Genesis 1:26 CSB:

> *"Then God said, 'Let us make man in our image, according to our likeness. They will rule the fish of the sea, the birds of the sky, the livestock, the whole earth, and the creatures that crawl on the earth.'"*

---

[3] "How Much of the Ocean Has Been Explored? - NOAA Ocean Exploration." *NOAA Ocean Exploration*, 28 Mar. 2025, oceanexplorer.noaa.gov/ocean-fact/explored/.

[4] Brennan, Pat. "Our Milky Way Galaxy: How Big Is Space? - NASA Science." *Science.nasa.gov*, 2 Apr. 2019, science.nasa.gov/universe/exoplanets/our-milky-way-galaxy-how-big-is-space/.

Our? as in plural?

Or when Jesus in John 10:30 CSB says,

"I and the Father are one."

Or one of the most memorized verses in the bible—Matthew 28:18-20 CSB,

"Jesus came near and said to them, 'All authority has been given to me in heaven and on earth. Go, therefore, and make disciples of all nations, baptizing them in the name of the Father and of the Son and of the Holy Spirit, teaching them to observe everything I have commanded you. And remember, I am with you always, to the end of the age.'"

The Bible clearly teaches that there is one God made up of three distinct persons—each 100% God on their own—unified in eternal loving union. He is both one *and* three, *three* and one. Despite all that we study and the insight we gather, this remains to be one of the great mysteries of faith. How is it possible? I like how A.W. Tozer grasps and comes to terms with the mystery when he says,

"The doctrine of the Trinity, as I have said before, is truth for the heart. The fact that it cannot be satisfactorily explained, instead of being against it, is in its favour. Such a truth had to be revealed; no one could have imagined

it"[5].

I have stopped trying to explain the Trinity perfectly. I let the mystery humble me—I find that the more I study the more I don't know. We don't drop our faith because we don't comprehend every nuance of theology. We keep discovering because what we find is so awe-inspiring that it transforms the very essence of our being.

The prophet Jeremiah, in the book of the same name, was placed in confinement for speaking out the words of God. Despite his imprisonment, God was still speaking to him. In Jeremiah 33:3 God tells him,

> *"Call to me and I will answer you and tell you great and incomprehensible things you do not know".*

The Hebrew word here used for *know* is the the word *Yada*[6]. The main definition for this word is *to know*; however, it's even deeper than just an intellectual knowing. It's experiential—the way you know yourself or the way you can know someone else relationally. In Genesis 4:1 NKJV, the word used to describe sexual relations when it says, "And the man *knew* Eve his wife, and she conceived and bore Cain".

To know something in this context is to know it intimately, with your heart, body and entire being, not just your mind. So when God tells Jeremiah that He wants tell him great and

---

[5] Tozer, A W. *KNOWLEDGE of the HOLY : The Attributes of God. Their Meaning in the Christian Life.* 2018.

[6] "know, v." The New Strong's Exhaustive Concordance of the Bible, Thomas Nelson, 2009, p. H3045.

incomprehensible things, He means that He wants to share with him all of the amazing and incredible things that man can not experience without the presence of God.

It doesn't say it here in the text but conceivably when we call out to God He could answer us with the mysteries of the depths of the oceans, the expanse of the universe, the Holy Spirit—or even the praying mantis. Not just to know the data but to experience, to know it as I know myself.

The invitation during our seasons of waiting is to pause, take notice, wonder, and experience. This can be as simple as closing our eyes and listening to the rustle of the leaves in the trees as the wind passes through. This can be as complicated as taking your entire family to the Scottish Highlands where you can stand in the moors in a torrential downpour—with your entire body soaked to its core. This could be a moment on your back porch, with your Bible realizing that the new covenant in Jesus' blood[7] mentioned in the Last Supper had its origins in Exodus[8] with the original covenant God made with His people. You know within your being that God is faithful to His people throughout all the ages and He will be to you.

Maybe that's what my son understood before I did. Waiting isn't wasted—it's an invitation to look closer, to wonder, to know God in the rustle of leaves and the stillness of a praying mantis—calling us to come and see. Maybe waiting is God's most tender classroom—the place where He teaches us not with answers, but with awe.

When we view waiting in this way, we have the opportunity to pause and see what is before us with clarity. We can meet with

---

[7] Luke 22:20 CSB

[8] Exodus 24:8 CSB

the presence of God—seek wisdom, holy creativity, and listen for the subtlety of His voice—so we can truly discern what He has for us in each and every moment.

* * *

Lord, teach us to see waiting as an adventure. Let us stop to take in the beauty of the trees, the wonder of the universe, the stillness of the praying mantis, the truth of who You truly are. Pull us out of the addictions we have to our phones, social media, jobs, and work. Help us to slow down and stand transfixed before your wondrous works.

In Jesus' Name,
Amen

* * *

Discussion Questions

- What's one way you can make responding in wonder and awe a daily habit of your mind?
- What is something you don't understand fully but you find awe inspiring?
- What do you think about the Hebrew word *yada* ('to know intimately')? How might this change the way you understand the word *know* in Scripture moving forward?

Chapter 2

The Tension

Isaiah, a prophet of the Lord, ends Isaiah Chapter 39 with a sobering pronouncement that one day the Babylonians would capture Jerusalem. This would come as quite a blow to Hezekiah (the king at the time) and the people of Judah. After all, only two chapters earlier in Isaiah 37, God had dramatically delivered Jerusalem from the Assyrian threat. How could the people of Judah celebrate the downfall of Assyria with a prophecy foretold of an even greater empire on the way?

This is where Isaiah shifts his tone to primarily comfort and blessing. He speaks encouragement to the faint and weary with this,

> "But those who wait on the Lord shall renew their strength; they shall mount up with wings like eagles, they shall run and not be weary, they shall walk and not faint" (Isaiah 40:31 NKJV).

In the Christian Standard Bible version, it says, "*But those who trust in the Lord*". Whether the translators used wait or trust, it comes from the same Hebrew word, *qāvâ.* The word occurs

49 times throughout the Old Testament. Its overall meaning according to Strong's Hebrew Dictionary[9], is "waiting for" but there is something much more interesting in the definition. This word most likely came from the base meaning to twist and stretch and then the tension that comes from it.

There is a tension that comes from waiting. It pulls you tight, makes you feel weak. The people of Judah had to wait with tension in their spirits for their holy city to be stripped of its possessions and its people. They didn't know when or how it would happen—only that God had spoken it. Yet Isaiah reminds them that waiting on the Lord is different. Waiting without trust twists you and makes you weak. It's the kind of tension that pulls you taut—the strain that makes you wonder if you might snap.

God doesn't promise that you will never feel that tension. He never says that you won't ever feel weary or weak. Even the strongest of us fail in our lives. It is a part of the human condition. The question is who will be the object you wait upon?

Will you allow your life to be dictated by fear, insecurity, pain, or the mistakes we all make?

Or will you step into a way of waiting that is filled with hope and anticipation? Another word the Bible uses for waiting is *yāḥal.* As with many other Hebrew words, *yāḥal* is much more than just waiting. Out of the 42 times this word is used in the Old Testament, approximately 32 of them are directed toward God as the object of the waiting. Even more importantly, the majority of the time scholars decided to translate this word as hope rather than wait or tarry. The Psalms are packed with moments where

---

[9] "Waiting for, v." The New Strong's Exhaustive Concordance of the Bible, Thomas Nelson, 2009, p. H6960.

the author waits and hopes in God.

David says in Psalm 31:24 "Be strong, and let your heart be courageous, all you who put your *hope* in the Lord."

And in Psalm 33:18, "May your faithful love rest on us, Lord, for we put our *hope* in you."

And Psalm 38:15, "For I put my *hope* in you, Lord; you will answer me, my Lord, my God."

Psalm 119:114, "You are my shelter and my shield; I put my *hope* in your word."

These words invite the reader into an active hope-filled kind of life; despite the stretching that occurs through difficult situations. This type of waiting doesn't stop in the book of Psalms. The people of Israel waited—generation after generation—for redemption, restoration and ultimately a savior. For centuries the people endured the Hebrew sense of *qāvâ*—to twist and stretch—in the spiritual tension of being pulled toward what God had promised, yet not seeing it fulfilled.

The people of Israel became living proof of the distinction between optimism and hope. Optimism looks at the possibility of something positive happening based on circumstances that have led up to this point. There is data trending toward that outcome, and therefore I can have faith that it will happen. Israel didn't have optimism. There was no reason to believe that they would come out of exile, end all oppression, return to their promised land, or receive the savior they had been promised. The data was not trending in their favor.

Isaiah says[10],

> *"The people walking in darkness*

---

[10] *Isaiah 9:2; 6-7 CSB*

have seen a great light;
a light has dawned
on those living in the land of darkness.
For a child will be born for us,
a son will be given to us,
and the government will be on his shoulders.
He will be named
Wonderful Counselor, Mighty God,
Eternal Father, Prince of Peace.
The dominion will be vast,
and its prosperity will never end.
He will reign on the throne of David
and over his kingdom,
to establish and sustain it
with justice and righteousness from now on and forever.
The zeal of the Lord of Armies will accomplish this."

Isaiah was not speaking of the Messiah out of optimism that He would come. They were still in darkness—no sight of dawn nor sign of deliverance. Isaiah, instead, was speaking from a hope that emerges when you turn your waiting toward God and His promises.

Later in Isaiah 25:9 CSB it says,

"On that day it will be said,
'Look, this is our God;
we have waited for him, and he has saved us.
This is the Lord; we have waited for him.
Let's rejoice and be glad in his salvation.'"

Their *qāvâ* for the Messiah was long and difficult. Some waited through oppression. Some in silence. The prophets spoke of Him as the coming King, suffering servant, the long awaited One, the Light in the darkness, and Emmanuel God with us. Some waited in exile and through many nights of unanswered prayers. But Isaiah looked at the wait in hopeful anticipation, believing that there would finally be a moment where the people of Israel would look upon Him with recognition. "He's the one we have been waiting for."

When Jesus finally did come, He didn't look as people expected. They thought He would be a warrior king but instead He was a baby in a manger. In Him was that waiting fulfilled. Hope had a name. The tension of generations finally had an answer—not the removal of all suffering but the Presence of God with His people.

The invitation God placed before the people of Israel is now presented before us—who or what will be the object of our waiting? Will we wait in apathy and complaining or will we wait in hopeful anticipation?

If you have been waiting—tired, stretched, overwhelmed, unsure where to place your hope—it's not too late and you are certainly not alone. There is a place for you. If you believe, you can place your hope in Him—Jesus the One who generations waited for, the One present with us today.

* * *

Lord, help us to put our hope in You. Every time we face struggles or difficulties, remind us that when You become the object of our waiting, we will be able to face anything that comes our way. Even when we cannot see the future, when it looks bleak, remind us of Your promises.

In Jesus' name,

Amen.

* * *

Discussion Questions

- *Have you ever felt stretched or pulled while waiting for what's next? How did that tension shape your faith?*
- *After learning the Hebrew words qāvâ and yāḥal more deeply, does it change the way you read Scripture?*
- *How will making God the object of your waiting impact the way you respond during this season of your life?*

Chapter 3

Breath of Renewal

While you wait personally, God wants to renew your strength, put the breath of His Spirit in your lungs. The word that the Hebrew people used to mean Spirit in the Old Testament is rûaḥ[11]. It's the word that is used to describe the Spirit of God that moved upon the face of the waters in Genesis 1:2. But that's not its only meaning. It means breath, the animating, energy-giving life to all living beings, and the wind that flows through the leaves on the trees. This Spirit that gave you life is now continually renewing you, putting breath into your lungs physically and spiritually.

Nearly a century after the prophecy given by Isaiah[12], the prophet Ezekiel was literally living within the fulfillment of that prophecy, standing amid the ruins of Isaiah's warning. Ezekiel was taken into exile in Babylon and there began his prophetic ministry. While there the people of Judah cried out,

---

[11] "Spirit, n." The New Strong's Exhaustive Concordance of the Bible, Thomas Nelson, 2009, p. H7307

[12] As referenced in chapter 2.

"Our bones are dried up, and our hope has perished;
we are cut off[13]."

God did not answer their despair with explanation alone—He answered it with a vision. This is what the prophet Ezekiel may have seen:

The luminance of the hand of the Lord hovered before me. I feared to take it, worried I would be shown more exile. I knew He wouldn't force me to take it, but somehow I knew I must. With that I reached out my hand, barely touching Him before I found myself standing in a valley.

The wind feels like a vortex around my face, blowing my hair to the side. There is a pit in my stomach growing more vast as I stare at the expanse of dead and dry bones as far as I can see. Silence filled the space, not a living soul. Devastation sets deep within me as I try to pick through the bones in front of me. There is no squeezing past them. It's like wading through an ocean of bones, never escaping them.

A pounding voice reverberates in my head, *"Son of man, can these bones live[14]?"*

My whole body quakes and I speak out as boldly as my voice will allow, *"Lord God, only you know[15]."*

The voice envelopes my mind again, *"Prophesy concerning these bones and say to them: Dry bones, hear the word of the Lord! This is what the Lord God says to these bones: I will cause breath to enter you, and you will live. I will put tendons on you, make flesh grow on you, and cover you with skin. I will put breath in you so*

---

[13] Ezekiel 37:11 CSB

[14] Ezekiel 37:3 CSB

[15] Ezekiel 37:3b CSB

that you come to life. Then you will know that I am the Lord[16] ."

So I spoke out the word of the Lord. As I was speaking, a rumble shook the ground I stood on. The bones began to rattle, hitting against each other, then flying to reach another bone of its match. Tendons came. Flesh and muscles began to creep over the bones like moss spreading across a stump. Skin wrapped them all but they laid motionless. They did not live. There was no breath in their lungs.

So the voice spoke again, *"Prophesy to the breath, prophesy, son of man. Say to it: This is what the Lord God says: Breath, come from the four winds and breathe into these slain so that they may live![17]"* So I spoke to the rûaḥ, the breath. And it came, filling the bodies of the slain, animating the lifeless and filling them with the rûaḥ, the Spirit, the life, the breath of the living God. A shuffle of movement began as each body rose to standing. A vast army, living and breathing as far as the eye could see.

I was jostled out of my shock by the voice of the Lord, *"Son of man, these bones are the whole house of Israel. Look how they say, 'Our bones are dried up, and our hope has perished; we are cut off.' Therefore, prophesy and say to them, 'This is what the Lord God says: I am going to open your graves and bring you up from them, my people, and lead you into the land of Israel. You will know that I am the Lord, my people, when I open your graves and bring you up from them. I will put my Spirit in you, and you will live, and I will settle you in your own land. Then you will know that I am the Lord. I have spoken, and I will do it. This is the declaration of the Lord[18] '.*"

---

[16] Ezekiel 37:4-6 CSB

[17] Ezekiel 37:9 CSB

[18] Ezekiel 37:11-14 CSB

* * *

The people of Israel had grown spiritually dry since their exile in Babylon. One could argue that it may have started even before then, a century earlier with the prophecy of Isaiah[19]. They felt dead in their devastation and grief but here God promises that He will bring life, renewal, restoration, and eventually be brought back into their land.

Do you feel dry and dead in your spirit? Do you need the rûaḥ, the Spirit of God, to fill those dead areas of your life? As you wait, do you feel weak and weary, like you won't be able to make it?

The voice of the living God is asking you to prophesy, speak over the dead, broken, weak, and weary portions of your life. He wants to give you His Spirit so that your bones come together, tendons, muscles, and skin revive your body. He wants to give you breath.

And when the Spirit breathes life into us, He does not merely revive us for *a moment*—He teaches us how to walk every step for the rest of our lives. In Galatians 5, the Apostle Paul is teaching the church how to walk by the Spirit opposed to the flesh. If you walk by the Spirit your life produces the fruit of the Spirit. In Galatians 5:22-25 CSB says,

> *"But the fruit of the Spirit is love, joy, peace, patience, kindness, goodness, faithfulness, gentleness, and self-control. The law is not against such things. Now those who belong to Christ Jesus have crucified the flesh with*

---

[19] As referenced in chapter 2.

its passions and desires. If we live by the Spirit, let us also keep in step with the Spirit."

When you are led and guided by the Spirit a singular unified character reflecting God's nature begins to emerge. The character that comes from living by the Spirit has qualities like love, joy, peace, patience, kindness, goodness, faithfulness, gentleness, self-control, and many more. The fruit is the *evidence* of a whole self that is transformed by the Spirit of the living God who dwells within us.

The world says create a habit — sprinkle a little love in this moment, a little joy here this week, some peace here and there, maybe some gentleness, but I'm not sure about self-control. If you put these habits into your life, according to the world, you should then become someone who lives by the Spirit. But the truth according to the Bible is the opposite — it says crucify your flesh, submit, rest, believe in Christ, give of yourself, and allow *His* presence to make a home in you, allow *Him* to do the work. *And then* you will be transformed by His Spirit and the fruit will become evident. The fruit of the Spirit doesn't grow because we try harder—it grows because we stay connected to the Spirit who lives within us.

In John 15:5 CSB Jesus says,

"I am the vine; you are the branches. The one who remains in me and I in him produces much fruit, because you can do nothing without me."

In order to see that transformation you must be connected. We have to get this in the correct order. First connection, then fruit—not the other way around.

As we stay connected to the Spirit, we begin to walk in step with the Spirit as referenced in Galatians 5:25. We walk at *His* pace and not at our own. There may be times that the pace is slower than we would like—maybe it feels like a standstill. But it's worth it. This type of waiting develops a sensitivity to the movements of the Spirit in our lives. When He steps, I step. When He stops, I stop—just as the people of Israel did in the wilderness when the glory cloud was guiding them. As Numbers 9:17 CSB says,

> *"Whenever the cloud was lifted up above the tent, the Israelites would set out; at the place where the cloud stopped, there the Israelites camped."*

The breath of the Spirit of God was working in the dead places in the people of Israel in the wilderness, while they were in exile in the book of Ezekiel, and He is now breathing into the dead places in your life as you walk with Him one step at a time. As you live this way day in, day out, the fruit of the Spirit then reveals itself throughout moments in your life when you would not have seen them before.

If you have not asked the Holy Spirit into your life or felt His presence lead you and guide you, then I leave that space for you here. Ask God to fill you with the Holy Spirit, His presence. This invitation isn't just for a chosen few—it's the promise Jesus gave to all who believe. Jesus told his disciples[20],

> "If you love me, you will keep my commands. And
> I will ask the Father, and he will give you another

---

[20] John 14:15–17a NKJV

Counselor to be with you forever. He is the Spirit of truth."

That same Spirit of Truth, the one who comforted and guided the disciples, is the very presence God offers to you today.

"How much more will your Father in heaven give the Holy Spirit to those who ask Him![21]

So ask Him.

* * *

Lord, breathe Your Spirit into the dry places of Your people today. Walk with them daily and gradually change their character to look more and more like You. I ask that You fill Your children reading this with Your Holy Spirit. Let the wind that blows through the trees and the oxygen that fills our lungs be a constant reminder of the renewal of life that You give us daily. You are as close as our breath.
In Jesus' name,
Amen.

* * *

Discussion Questions

- What areas of your life feel dry, weary, or lifeless right now? What might it look like to invite the breath of God into those

---

[21] *Luke 11:13 NKJV*

spaces?

- Have you ever invited the Holy Spirit to fill and lead your life? How have you experienced His presence or renewal?
- Which fruit of the Spirit feels most natural? Which feels most challenging? What can you do to invite the Spirit into those challenging places?

Chapter 4

Waiting with a New Song

I ran my thumb over the next large, smooth stone in my hand, and it brought back the memory. This was the stone for the teaching job I was not credentialed to have. I shouldn't have gotten it, but the Lord provided in a way only He can. I hold onto it a moment longer. The warm breeze flows through my hair, moving it from side to side. Mist from the roaring river beside me sprinkles onto my arms and face. I close my eyes and let these feelings wash over me. "Thank you, Lord," I whisper as I bend down and put the rock in its place. These weren't literal stones; the river was not actually before me, but images I held with God in my heart. These inner stones were moments of remembrance where I had seen God move in my life.

I continue along the riverbed, one rock at a time in remembrance. I place one for the years I waited for my husband. I was not patient in my waiting and I made so many mistakes but God was faithful. I hop over rocks to avoid getting my feet wet as I place the stone for Charlie, my son, remembering a time when I did not know if he would ever come. A smile spreads across my face for Theodore as I picture his toothless infant grin in my mind's eye, and I place the stone.

I reach the last stone I have and I'm pulled back into the memory that repeated itself over and over. Sometimes I talked with a friend, drove, or lay in bed crying out to God in the dark. While pregnant with Theodore, a single thought often brought me to tears. I had enough disability to cover the first six weeks of life but after that my job would only pay a small portion of my income during baby bonding. Our finances might force me to return to work, attempting to teach while my 6 week old infant was in the arms of someone else. That was something I just could not fathom. While I didn't yet know his face, I would dream of him. This is where, time and time again, I would cry out to the Lord. I told Him again and again my need. He would have to do what I could not. In my own ability, I did not see a way but God had done the miraculous time after time. My life was full of moments when God made a way where I saw none. So I waited.

Out of that waiting came a song, figuratively flowing out as an expression of the heart that bursts forth—one that flowed through my life and spilled from my lips to everyone I knew. God would make a way, just as He had before—beyond anything I could accomplish on my own. This song came out of a place of remembrance, a place of faith.

As I placed my stones of remembrance, I thought of another riverbed—one where God's people once crossed from wilderness to promise. After traveling in the desert for forty years, the people of Israel were ready to cross the Jordan River into the promised land. The trouble was that it was harvest season and the Jordan overflowed its banks during that time; creating a river likely measuring more than 300 feet across and over 10 feet deep.[22] This would have proven to be almost impossible with the several million Israelites loaded down with their livestock, children, elderly, and household goods without the hand of God. Joshua believed that God would do the miraculous.

God spoke through Joshua saying,

> "You will know that the living God is among you and that He will certainly dispossess before you the Canaanites, Hethites, Hivites, Perizzites, Girgashites, Amorites, and Jebusites when the ark of the covenant of the Lord of the whole earth goes ahead of you into the Jordan. Now choose twelve men from the tribes of Israel, one man for each tribe. When the feet of the priests who carry the ark of the Lord, the Lord of the whole earth, come to rest in the Jordan's water, its water will be cut off. The water flowing downstream will stand up in a mass" (Joshua 3:10-13 CSB).

God was going to go against the enemies of His people to provide for them the promised land. Canaanites are driven out. Hethites are driven out. Hivites are driven out. Perizzites are driven out. Girgashites are driven out. Amorites are driven out. Jebusites are driven out. In the same way God cleared the land before Israel, He clears the obstacles before us—not always instantly, but faithfully, in His time. This is the type of word the Lord wants to speak over your enemies. Anxiety is driven out. Depression is driven out. Anger is driven out. Poverty is driven out. Sickness

---

[22] Constable, Thomas. DD. "Commentary on Joshua 3". "Dr. Constable's Expository Notes". https://www.studylight.org/commentaries/eng/dcc/joshua-3.html?utm_source=chatgpt.com. 2012.

is driven out. Hopelessness is driven out. He will ultimately dispossess the enemies before you, just as He did for the people of Israel.

The water continued to surge past the people of Israel being the wall that kept them from their promise until the toes of the priests holding the Ark of the Covenant of the Lord touched the water. Then the water flowing downstream froze in place, standing still before the people. The mass of water rose up as far as 15 to 20 miles upstream in the city of Adam[23]. Imagine those people standing on the banks miles upstream where the water was held in place. Or the people downstream near the Dead Sea. Water is no longer flowing. This is the type of miracle no one could miss.

The priests with the Ark of the Covenant stood as a barricade holding the weight of tons of water as the people of Israel crossed from one side of the Jordan to the other. The sun set before all of the people made it across. Then Joshua commanded that twelve men would be selected, one from each tribe to select a stone from the center of the river and bring it to the other side. Joshua also set up twelve stones in the middle of the river. Only when the priests stepped onto the far bank did the waters rush forward again, resuming their course as before.

There were several purposes for these memorial stones. They were to stand as a remembrance of God's power. He was able to stop the flow of water from the Jordan revealing His might and His ability to fulfill His promises to the people of Israel, bring them into the promised land.

---

[23] Constable, Thomas. DD. "Commentary on Joshua 3". "Dr. Constable's Expository Notes". https://www.studylight.org/commentaries/eng/dcc/joshua-3.html?utm_source=chatgpt.com. 2012.

> "For the Lord your God dried up the water of the Jordan before you until you had crossed over, just as the Lord your God did to the Red Sea, which He dried up before us until we had crossed over. This is so that all the peoples of the earth may know that the Lord's hand is strong, and so that you may always fear the Lord your God" (Joshua 4:23-24 CSB).

These stones were to bring glory to the Lord from all nations. There is no way that the surrounding peoples would have missed this miracle and therefore it was a reminder to them of the power of God as well.

Another purpose of the memorial stones is to teach future generations of God's miraculous acts. God intended the people of Israel to tell their children and their children's children for generations the acts of the almighty God, how He brought them out of slavery in Egypt and then led them over the Jordan River into the land that was promised to them.

> "And he said to the Israelites, 'In the future, when your children ask their fathers, 'What is the meaning of these stones?' you should tell your children, 'Israel crossed the Jordan on dry ground'" (Joshua 4:21-22).

As we place our personal stones of remembrance, let us also be able to say, this is what miraculous things God has done when our children ask us.

The final purpose of the memorial stones is to mark a new beginning for the people of Israel. Crossing the Jordan River was a symbol of their transition from wandering in the desert for forty years to inheritance; from promise to possession. These stones were a reminder of God's covenant with the people of Israel. With the act of placing each stone, a song of deliverance rose up as a sweet incense to the Lord—not literal voices but an act of worship presented by action through faith. This worship was given for the miraculous God had already done over and over. The deliverance from Egypt. The provision in the desert. The crossing of the Jordan. But this worship also went up to the ears of God for what He had not yet done. The enemies of the people of Israel were not yet removed but remembrance was placed in the knowledge that if God could do all the things He had already done then He could most certainly move the enemies from their place before His people.

Songs of deliverance, redemption, and thanksgiving have flowed from the pages of the Bible reminding the people of God His acts in the past and what will come in the future in faith. When we've seen God's faithfulness and stand at the edge of what's next, the right response is worship. David once wrote a song from that very place — a new song that rose out of his waiting. As you read Psalm 40, note the progression of David's writing. He first stands in remembrance of a past deliverance. He remembers how in the past the Lord heard his cry and rescued him. Following that salvation, David praised the Lord. David then speaks out how he decides to act in response to God's faithfulness. Finally, David brings his present need for deliverance to the Lord. He is speaking out his petition to the Lord because he remembers another time when he was delivered.

Psalm 40 CSB

I waited patiently for the Lord,
   and He turned to me and heard my cry for help.
   He brought me up from a desolate pit,
   out of the muddy clay,
   and set my feet on a rock,
   making my steps secure.
   He put a new song in my mouth,
   a hymn of praise to our God.
   Many will see and fear,
   and they will trust in the Lord.

How happy is anyone
   who has put his trust in the Lord
   and has not turned to the proud
   or to those who run after lies!
   Lord my God, you have done many things—
   your wondrous works and your plans for us;
   none can compare with you.
   If I were to report and speak of them,
   they are more than can be told.

You do not delight in sacrifice and offering;
   you open my ears to listen.
   You do not ask for a whole burnt offering or a sin
offering.
   Then I said, "See, I have come;
   in the scroll it is written about me.
   I delight to do your will, my God,
   and your instruction is deep within me."

I proclaim righteousness in the great assembly;

see, I do not keep my mouth closed—
as you know, Lord.
I did not hide your righteousness in my heart;
I spoke about your faithfulness and salvation;
I did not conceal your constant love and truth
from the great assembly.

Lord, you do not withhold your compassion from me.
Your constant love and truth will always guard me.
For troubles without number have surrounded me;
my iniquities have overtaken me; I am unable to see.
They are more than the hairs of my head,
and my courage leaves me.
Lord, be pleased to rescue me;
hurry to help me, Lord.

Let those who intend to take my life
be disgraced and confounded.
Let those who wish me harm
be turned back and humiliated.
Let those who say to me, "Aha, aha!"
be appalled because of their shame.

Let all who seek you rejoice and be glad in you;
let those who love your salvation continually say,
"The Lord is great!"
I am oppressed and needy;
may the Lord think of me.
You are my helper and my deliverer;
my God, do not delay.

The Lord put a new song in the heart of David as He rescued him from His enemies. The Lord wants to give you a new song in your heart as you wait for Him. As you wait for each of the situations in your life. Sing a new song of the places of remembrance; all the things the Lord has done. Sing a new song of all you believe He will do in the future. Sing as the four living creatures and twenty-four elders, falling before the Lord.

> "And they sang a new song: You are worthy to take the scroll and to open its seals, because you were slaughtered, and you purchased people for God by your blood from every tribe and language and people and nation" (Revelation 5:9 CSB).

Join all of heaven in celebrating Jesus's redemptive work. And take the advice of Paul the Apostle and,

> "give thanks in everything; for this is God's will for you in Christ Jesus" (1 Thessalonians 5:18 CSB).

Sing, give thanks and then, like David, you can ask for His next act of deliverance with the faith of someone whose seen it before. With each stone of remembrance, your song is rising up to heaven giving praise and thanksgiving to the King and in the process reminding yourself what He can and will do in your life!

I kept up my song and in the final moments of my pregnancy God answered me in a way I could never have accomplished on my own. At the time, my husband worked as a security guard at a school. He loved his job, but it didn't pay enough for me to stay home with our baby. One day he came home from work, telling me that he had decided he was going to apply to be a special education teacher or a resource teacher. I was surprised to say the least. These positions require you to have a teaching credential that takes a couple of years to receive after more schooling but he applied and signed up for classes. He stepped forward, interviewed, and the district offered him the job. There would be no way for me to be sitting with my infant, writing a book on waiting if it weren't for the powerful intervention of God.

With that realization, I place my last stone of remembrance. Tears pour down my face as I lift my praises up to the King. This time there is no whispering. There is only a shout of thanksgiving toward heaven.

Both—a song and the stones—stand as a figurative representation of my thankfulness for all that God has done and the steps forward I can now take because of the faith that now exists. What are the stones of remembrance in your own life — the moments where God made a way? Lay them out before you, either in your mind or in writing and then give Him thanks.

* * *

Waiting is worship.

* * *

Lord, I thank you for all that you have already done in the lives of the people reading. I praise you for their life and I ask that as they sing their songs of remembrance out to You that You would provide for them during their waiting. I pray that you would move back the waters of their lives and create a space for them to walk about on dry land and years from now they would be able to tell their children of Your goodness.

In Jesus' name,

Amen

* * *

Discussion Questions

- God promised to drive out Israel's enemies before them. What enemies in your own life do you need Jesus to drive out today?
- Take time to write out your stones of remembrance— moments when God showed up in your life in miraculous ways. How can these stones shape the way you wait now?
- In what ways is waiting a form of worship? How can remembering what God has done strengthen your song in the waiting?

Chapter 5

At the Feet of Jesus

For the most part, waiting is something that is forced upon us. It's something that happens *to* us. But have you ever experienced a moment when you decided to put yourself into a place of waiting?

Many times it takes great discernment and self-control to pull yourself back from something you want to pursue. But when you choose to hold yourself back and follow the voice of God, there is something valuable for you on the other end.

I felt this most strongly prior to the birth of my oldest son. He was what the doctors would consider post term. Every time I had an appointment the doctors would tell me that it was time for my induction. Granted there are times when inductions are medically necessary but I was low risk and there was no indication that anything was wrong. I prayed and sought the voice of God and I felt very strongly that I was supposed to wait for Charlie to come in his own timing. Every day felt like weeks—waiting despite what others had to say.

Those weeks in the waiting that I chose felt like the longest moments of my life but I learned how to trust God in a way I never had before. It brings the scripture Proverbs 3:5-6 CSB into a new light when it says,

> *"Trust in the Lord with all your heart,*
>   *and do not rely on your own understanding;*
>   *in all your ways know him,*
>   *and he will make your paths straight."*

And when Charlie was born healthy, the most observant kid I'd ever seen, I knew then with all my heart and soul that God was trustworthy in my life. It wasn't just a fact I learned but an experience that changed me. I revisit those moments often. It allows me to trust Him in my current situation and many more to come.

Waiting teaches you many valuable lessons. Like me, it can teach you trust, strengthen relationships, and reorder your priorities but the most important thing we can learn in our waiting is the heart and identity of Jesus Himself.

Learning the character of a person can take a lifetime. When you're in a relationship you can learn something new about that person even when you are old and gray. This is even more true about Jesus. When we spend time in Scripture, we are putting ourselves into a position to learn more and develop a deeper relationship with Him.

Scholars often view Scripture as Jewish meditation literature[24]. It's not meant to be read once and then left like other literature. It's meant to be read, contemplated, prayed, memorized over a lifetime. One of the simplest ways we practice

---

[24] Collins, Jon and Mackie, Tim, hosts. "The Bible as Jewish Meditation Literature - Jewish Scripture Meditation vs. Modern Meditation". *The Bible Project*, August 11, 2018. https://bibleproject.com/podcasts/how-read-bible-part-6-jewish-scripture-meditation-vs-modern-meditation/

this kind of waiting is through silence and solitude. If your life is consumed by noise, you can choose silence —putting away your phones, your tasks, even your words— to create space for connection with the Holy Spirit. Silence is not empty; it is active. Building relationship with Him through your time.

Psalm 1 says this about the ideal Bible reader,

> *"Blessed is the man...[whose] delight is in the law of the Lord, and in His law he meditates day and night"* (Psalm *1:1a; 2 NKJV).*

Waiting is not a waste of time. When we are forced to wait, we are given the gift of time—moments we can put ourselves at the feet of Jesus, listening and learning just like Mary.

Mary, Martha, and their brother Lazarus were great friends and followers of Jesus. He would come and visit them in Bethany often. They are mentioned in New Testament scriptures in three separate stories.

In Luke 10:38-42, Mary is sitting at the feet of Jesus while her sister Martha is busy making preparations for the visitors. Martha complains to Jesus that her sister is leaving her to do all the work. In response Jesus says,

> *"Martha, Martha, you are worried and upset about many things, but one thing is necessary. Mary has made the right choice, and it will not be taken away from her"* (Luke *10:41-42 CSB).*

Mary's choice was not passive. It was one made in submission. Like Mary, we can set aside moments to remove the hurry from our lives. While technology is a powerful addition to our lives, it has also contributed to a hurried, stressed, and anxiety-filled society unlike any before it. As hard as it may be to hear, maybe our modern *right choice* is moments of Jesus over our phones. Even short moments of submission can change how we interact with Jesus.

Mary presents herself as someone who values sitting at the feet of Jesus. Scripture reveals Jesus as many things—Savior, Redeemer, King, Servant, Son of God, and Son of Man but he was also known to the people of this time as a Rabbi. A Rabbi is a teacher of the Torah, the law. In Hebrew, it literally means "my teacher" or "my master"[25]. According to the book, "Sitting at the Feet of Rabbi Jesus" by Ann Spangler and Lois Tverberg, Mary was sitting at the feet of Jesus as would other disciples or students at the time.

> *"It was customary for rabbis to sit on low pillows or chairs while they were teaching. Their disciples would sit on the ground or on mats around them. That's how the phrase 'sit at his feet' became an idiom for learning from a rabbi"*[26].

She desired to learn not only what Jesus knew but His character. We know this was her continual practice because of another story we read about her.

In John 12:1-8, Jesus was about a week away from his crucifix-

---

[25] MJL. "What Does It Mean to Be a Rabbi?" *My Jewish Learning*, My Jewish Learning, 30 Apr. 2003, www.myjewishlearning.com/article/rabbi-teacher -preacher-judge-but-not-priest/.

[26] Spangler, Ann, and Lois Tverberg. *Sitting at the Feet of Rabbi Jesus : How the Jewishness of Jesus Can Transform Your Faith.* Grand Rapids, Michigan, Zondervan, 2018, Page 18.

ion when He stopped in Bethany at the home of Lazarus, Martha, and Mary. As Jesus was sitting and teaching, Mary

> *"took a pound of perfume, pure and expensive nard, anointed Jesus's feet, and wiped his feet with her hair. So the house was filled with the fragrance of the perfume"* (John 12:3 CSB).

Despite the complaints of Judas and probably the shock of the other disciples, Jesus reveals one facet of her act as a preparation for His burial but there was something else Mary may have been saying. During the time Mary had been learning at the feet of Jesus, she had come to believe this about Him—that He was the Messiah or "anointed one". Anointing was used throughout Scripture to set someone apart, like priests and kings. Kings like Saul, David, and Solomon were anointed and set apart for God's work to lead the people. Not only would this happen when they were crowned but it was general practice for kings to wear expensive oils on their bodies and clothes[27].

What is Mary saying as she anoints Jesus' feet with this expensive oil? After all her hours spent sitting at the feet of her Rabbi—listening, asking, waiting—what had she learned about Jesus?

Her acts spoke of Jesus as King!

This anointing was an act of faith that reverberated in the week to come. From here Jesus purposed Himself to ride into Jerusalem but this time wasn't like the other times He had entered Jerusalem. Jesus commissioned His disciples to untie a donkey to bring it to Him fulfilling the prophecy from Zechariah

---

[27] Spangler and Tverberg, 22.

9:9 CSB,

> *"Rejoice greatly, Daughter Zion!*
>   *Shout in triumph, Daughter Jerusalem!*
>   *Look, your King is coming to you;*
>   *he is righteous and victorious,*
>   *humble and riding on a donkey,*
>   *on a colt, the foal of a donkey".*

Entering Jerusalem from the East, the Mount of Olives, fulfilling the prophecy in Zechariah 14:4 CSB,

> *"On that day his feet will stand on the Mount of Olives,*
> *which faces Jerusalem on the east".*

Riding down the same way as another king in 1 Kings 1:38-40,

> *"Then the priest Zadok, the prophet Nathan, Benaiah*
> *son of Jehoiada, the Cherethites, and the Pelethites went*
> *down, had Solomon ride on King David's mule, and took*
> *him to Gihon. The priest Zadok took the horn of oil from*
> *the tabernacle and anointed Solomon. Then they blew*
> *the ram's horn, and all the people proclaimed, "Long live*
> *King Solomon!" All the people went up after him, playing*
> *flutes and rejoicing with such a great joy that the earth*
> *split open from the sound".*

All of this He did while smelling like a king[28], with the anointing fresh from Mary's faithful act. And the people took notice

---

[28] Spangler and Tverberg, 22.

shouting,

> "Hosanna *to the Son of David!*
> *Blessed is he who comes in the name*
> *of the Lord!*
> Hosanna *in the highest heaven!"* (*Matthew* 21:9 *CSB*)

They recognized Him as the King—the long-awaited Messiah, the Anointed One promised centuries before. The rest of the week Jesus went from crying out to God in the Garden of Gethsemane, to being interrogated by priests and Pilate, to being tortured and crucified all while smelling like the King, anointed by someone who knew Him for what He was.

This is an invitation for you to spend your seasons of waiting at the feet of Jesus—learning from Scripture His acts, what He spoke, the scriptures He read in the Old Testament, all while learning about His heart for you. That kind of waiting is not a waste, it is a gift from God Almighty for you to learn all you can about the King above every other king. And even now, our prayers, moments of silence, our waiting, our choice to listen to Scripture slowly, and our resistance to hurry rise like that fragrance before our King.

* * *

Lord, I pray that we wouldn't take these moments of waiting for granted. Give us the strength and obedience to wait when you tell us—choosing Your way. I ask that You would help us to use them as an opportunity to get to know You more—not only as our King but as our friend. Teach us how to sit at Your feet like Mary did, learning about You and then taking all we have learned and putting it into action.

> *In Jesus' Name,*
> *Amen*

* * *

Discussion Questions

- Can you think of a time when waiting taught you a valuable lesson?
- What is something you learned about Jesus because of the time you've taken to read Scripture?
- How can you live out what you've learned about Him in your daily life?

Chapter 6

Binding Service

Not a single trickle remained in the brook where Elijah had once knelt to drink. What was once flowing, had run dry as the time without rain went from days to months. Elijah laid himself flat so his forehead was placed beneath the faint trace of shade from the Ar'ar bush. God had not spoken what to do next, so he waited. Devastation in his heart poured like the sweat on his brow.

The black pointed beak of the raven appeared between the branches and dropped the bread and meat the Lord had commanded. It was the *just enough* of the desert—but the absence of water was beginning to be felt.

The powerful Voice Elijah relied on surged through his mind, *"Get up, go to Zarephath that belongs to Sidon and stay there. Look, I have commanded a woman who is a widow to provide for you there.*[29]*"*

The command felt strange. *A widow? The most vulnerable—the poorest will provide? A gentile will give to a prophet of Yahweh?*

He had no option but to obey. The Word of drought he spoke

---

[29] 1 Kings 17:9 CSB

weighed heavily upon his heart.

* * *

Her god, Baal, had not provided. The jar of flour held only dregs—the oil, just a few drops. Her thoughts ran through her mind as she picked up one stick, then another, and another at the city gate, *this is the last of it—we're done.* A sob catches in her throat at the thought of her son dead. There was nothing left after this, and surely no one was coming to her rescue.

* * *

That must be her, Elijah thought as his throbbing foot took another step toward the city.

The woman at the gate was gaunt, *worse than me.* Her hands shook as she bent over to pick up one stick after another—her breathing slow and labored. *Lord, are You sure this is the woman who will help me?*

As he reached her he spoke softly his request, *"Please bring me a little water in a cup and let me drink.*[30]*"*

Despite her apparent hunger, she looked at him with what seemed like curiosity. She turned and brought him the water that he requested. *Maybe this would work.*

With a gulp of the water came his second request, *"Please bring me a piece of bread in your hand*[31]*."*

---

[30] 1 Kings 17:10 CSB

[31] 1 Kings 17:11 CSB

* * *

Can this man not see that I'm starving? Does he not know that I cannot even feed myself or my family?

The words come out stronger than she feels, "As the Lord your God lives, I don't have anything baked—only a handful of flour in the jar and a bit of oil in the jug. Just now, I am gathering a couple of sticks in order to go prepare it for myself and my son so we can eat it and die.[32]" Her voice stumbled over the last word.

* * *

The fear I hear in her voice is the same fear I carry every day. This drought came from my mouth. Yet God...

He takes a step toward her, placing a hand on her shoulder, "Don't be afraid; go and do as you have said. But first make me a small loaf from it and bring it out to me. Afterward, you may make some for yourself and your son, for this is what the Lord God of Israel says, 'The flour jar will not become empty and the oil jug will not run dry until the day the Lord sends rain on the surface of the land[33].'"

* * *

What if this is true? What if I give the last of what I have? It's a

---

[32] 1 Kings 17:12 CSB

[33] 1 Kings 17:13-14 CSB

risk—but she decides to serve.

* * *

Elijah watches as the widow kneads the dough. Prayers flow through his mind with each stretch of the dough. *Lord, please provide. Lord, follow through with Your promises. Lord, help us.*

* * *

Her stomach tightens as she pours the oil. Every drop feels like a death—and yet somehow, also like a faith she didn't know she had. She kneads the dough with trembling hands. Each movement feels like surrender. *This is all I have—yet I'm giving it away.* Her service becomes her offering.

She watches the man place the last of what she has in his mouth. Desperation filling her body. *What if this works? What if it doesn't?*

* * *

Day after day, the miracle renews itself. The widow opens the jar and flour remains. The oil is continually poured out. The widow eats. Her son eats. And Elijah eats.

Both the widow and Elijah are in waiting. The widow waits for death—in hopelessness. Elijah waits for the next command; he waits for the rain. Their waiting seasons intertwine—each sustains the other through acts of obedience and service. God often sustains His people through *mutual acts of service* even when both parties feel empty. In this story:

The widow gives bread; Elijah gives God's word.

She meets a physical need; he meets a spiritual one.

Both are filled—physically, emotionally, and spiritually—*in the act of serving during the wait.* Their shared obedience became a living parable of what God does when His people serve one another. And their story invites us to consider: what might God do in *our* waiting if we serve as they did?

During our times of waiting, God may place before us an opportunity to serve someone else. Maybe we do as James 1:27 suggests and, "*care for orphans and widows in their distress.*" This could mean bringing food to someone's house or throwing a Christmas party with presents for orphans with no family to do this for them.

This could be as simple as listening to your co-worker as they express their devastation over their divorce and speaking hope and life into their situation.

Maybe this is serving in your local church. You agree to pray with your fellow congregants after the service ends, you join the tech team, feed others with the hospitality team or weekly food pantry, or clean the bathrooms. Whatever your gifting or capability—you serve.

Through these acts of service you may come to receive exactly what you need during your waiting. As you give to God's people you may come to realize you are being served as well, your heart being filled, your spirit revived.

Some of the most fulfilling times in my life have been serving others on missions in countries like Myanmar and Thailand. Oftentimes we would go with the intention of providing a health clinic. As someone who has no medical experience, I would end up doing everything else, which included purchases and stocking medicines, running around like an errand girl, and of course praying.

It's incredible to me because the point is for us to go and serve the people, which we do but so often I also get served in the process. I can think of a time where we were at the end of our clinic, resting from the frantic work and a man told us of the pain in his body. One of his legs was in fact longer than the other and so it caused all sorts of pain in his body.

And so we prayed. We prayed for his healing, we prayed, in Jesus' name that this leg would grow to the correct size. And it did.

That fact still amazes me to this day.

How could you see something so miraculous and not be changed and moved? I came home from that trip spiritually full—my faith reinvigorated and my heart changed.

As we serve, we come to find that it's not the actual things we do for each other—it's that the acts are given from the heart in compassion and mutual understanding. What happens within our hearts as we serve is the actual miracle.

One of my favorite books is called *Tattoos on the Heart: The Power of Boundless Compassion*[34]. It is a memoir written by a Jesuit Priest, Greg Boyle, who serves gang members in Los Angeles. One of Boyle's beliefs is the profound impact that unconditional love and compassion has—seeing and accepting those that live in the margins of society. In a TED Talk[35] in 2012

---

[34] Boyle, Gregory. *Tattoos on the Heart: The Power of Boundless Compassion.* New York, NY, Free Press, 2011.

[35] TEDx Talks. "Compassion and Kinship: Fr Gregory Boyle at TEDxConejo 2012." *YouTube*, 20 June 2012, www.youtube.com/watch?v=ipRokWt1Fkc.

he talks about kinship in this way,

> *"How we achieve a certain type of companionship that stands in awe of what the poor have to carry rather than stand in judgment at how they carry it. For the measure of our compassion lies not in our service of those on the margins but in our willingness to see ourselves in kinship with them in mutuality."*

Our service pours into both those serving and those being served through our communion with each other.

* * *

The story of Elijah and the widow continue when her son becomes ill and then dies. The woman comes before Elijah in distress demanding to know what he has done to stand against her that her son would die.

Elijah brought the boy before the Lord crying out to Him, "Lord my God, have you also brought tragedy on the widow I am staying with by killing her son?[36]"

Elijah and this woman carry a story of mutual compassion and kinship. They each served each other in order that they both may survive. This binding between souls created within Elijah the faith to ask something unprecedented. He had seen God have the power over life and death when He fed him with food provided by ravens and then the unending flour and oil provided by the poor widow. And so he cried out in compassion, desperation, true faith and service to the woman and said, "*Lord*

____

[36] 1 Kings 17:20 CSB

my God, please let this boy's life come into him again![37]"

In the first time in all of scripture, breath enters the lungs of the boy and he lives—resurrected from death.

The binding service that brought the dead to life also did something else miraculous. When this woman sees her son alive she says to Elijah, *"Now I know you are a man of God and the Lord's word from your mouth is true[38]."*

Salvation reaches a gentile woman living on the margins of society—poor pagan widow—through the mutual service with a prophet of Israel. They should not have had any relationship but when they gave they were changed with pure compassion and hope.

Your service can do the same. It can bring you into relationship with the poor and hurting—following the commands of Jesus to care for the marginalized. By doing so it can also give you direction, revive you and perform the miraculous in your life.

* * *

Lord, give us compassion for the hungry, poor and marginalized. Help us to create a binding mutuality that stirs a desire to serve others, and as we serve, speak to our hearts—giving us the answers we need in our seasons of waiting. Allow our ears to be open to Your voice as You lead us toward those who need Your love and salvation.

In Jesus' name,

Amen.

* * *

---

[37] 1 Kings 17:21b CSB

[38] 1 Kings 17:24 CSB

Discussion Questions

- In the story of Elijah and the widow, what do you think is the most powerful lesson?
- What are some ways that come to your mind where you could be of service?
- How does the command to serve those on the margins make you feel? Does it make you uncomfortable, inspired, or hesitant? What might your reaction reveal about your heart?

Chapter 7

Out of Egypt, Out of Emptiness

The sweltering Egyptian sun watches the work from high above the desert plain. The temples and pyramids hover hazily in the distance taking up the entire skyline. Aaron, holder of the beloved Hebrew name, exalted, plunges his hands into the mud again. His feet hidden below the mud squelch as the water and dirt slide between his toes. Sweat slides down his forehead into his eyes blurring his vision—yet he continues.

The crack of the whip echoes near his ear and he pushes his already broken body to the edge. A groan rumbles through his chest and he cries out, "Oh Lord, don't forget us!"

> "The Israelites groaned because of their difficult labor, and they cried out; and their cry for help ascended to God because of the difficult labor. So God heard their groaning, and He remembered His covenant with Abraham, Isaac, and Jacob"[39].

---

[39] Exodus 2:23–24 CSB

And so God heard the cry of Aaron and the rest of his people and sent a deliverer in the form of Moses. We can pick up the story that is central to the Jewish faith at the tenth and final plague in the Exodus story. God moved to take His people out of the oppression they had endured for 400 years. If we pause for a moment to consider what that amount of time meant to these people—continued generations of slaves. Their identity rose and fell by how much they could work and what they could produce. If they couldn't produce, their life was worthless. The survival of their entire family was based on their work.

Now we have God, and not just any god but the Elohim above all other elohim, the God above every other god, even the gods Pharaoh believed in, coming to the aid of these people. And here we are at the last plague. God says He will bring a plague on all of Egypt that will kill every firstborn son. Pharaoh had a chance to stop the cry of anguish that was about to pour out over Egypt but he wouldn't.

But this isn't Pharaoh's story. It is the story of the birth of a people. The instructions that God gave to Moses and the Hebrew people were to slaughter a lamb and spread its blood over the doorposts. In this way the angel would know to pass over those households.

This moment marks the first symbol of birth in the story. When we are born into this world, we leave the womb we are living in, the only place we have ever known and we are literally ejected through blood and water, pushed out into a whole new world.

The Hebrew people were first pressed out of a bloody door into a world they had never known before by the power of God. Then they were followed by Pharaoh to the Red Sea where they passed through the waters to a place Pharaoh could never get them. This moment of deliverance was not just an escape—it was a birth story written in blood and water.

Just as we are birthed out of our mothers, this was the birth of a people, fashioned after God's own heart.

This is not the only place in the Bible where birth is used to tell a greater story. The Bible grapples with the pain and loss of barrenness repeatedly.

For those who have faced the loss of a child or the inability to carry one, this moment is for you. I can't begin to know the plan that God has for each and every one of you but I do know that God was faithful all through the pages of the Bible to every woman facing a similar situation and He will also be faithful to you.

We can go all the way back to the patriarchs of our faith. Sarah, the wife of Abraham, was barren for decades. It has even been suggested by Torah scholars that Abraham knew that she was barren before he married her and yet in his faithfulness to God, he still did the right thing by her. It took them well into their senior years to finally bear a son. Or what about Rebekah, the wife of Isaac, who was barren for 20 years? Or Rachel who was overshadowed by her sister Leah? Or even Elizabeth, the mother of John the Baptist, was elderly and had not had a child until John? Over and over again these women were physically unable to produce life in their womb but God intervened and performed the miraculous, in His timing, for His purposes.

These ancient stories were written in a time when society did not value the lives and stories of women. Despite this, these women are not only in the story but they hold primary roles in moving forward God's redemptive plan for His people.

There is one woman that I want to highlight in particular, her name is Hannah.

The woman knelt on the temple steps, tears streaming down her cheeks. Red surrounded her eyes and nose. Her lips muttered under her breath unintelligible whispers. Drops made their way to the stone steps. Drop, drop, one at a time staining the gray underneath her.

She struggles with the words, *"Lord of Armies, if you take notice of your servant's affliction, remember and not forget me, and give your servant a son, I will give him to the Lord all the days of his life, and his hair will never be cut[40]"*.

Eli the priest was perched on his seat of authority, a stool looking down on the woman, eyes squinting toward her muttering below. A sigh pressed through his nostrils. *"How long are you going to be drunk? Get rid of your wine[41]!"*, he declared.

Eyes wide as tears continued to fall unchecked down her face. *"No, my lord! I am a woman with a broken heart. I haven't had any wine or beer; I've been pouring out my heart before the Lord. Don't think of me as a wicked woman; I've been praying from the depth of anguish and resentment[42]"*, she cried out.

The lines on his forehead and around his eyes soften. He looks to her with compassion, *"Go in peace, and may the God of Israel grant the request you've made of Him[43]"*.

Society expected Hannah to dwell in her grief silently. It viewed her inability to bear children as a curse, as if she had done something to deserve such a fate. Instead of doing what was expected, she petitioned God. She took all of her grief and sorrow and brought it before the Lord, begging Him to hear her

---

[40] 1 Samuel 1:11 CSB

[41] 1 Samuel 1:14 CSB

[42] 1 Samuel 1:15-16 CSB

[43] 1 Samuel 1:17 CSB

request. Just as the Lord heard a nation's cry for deliverance, so did He hear the cries of an individual woman whose womb was shut.

For nineteen years, Hannah waited and wept before the Lord, and for four hundred years, Israel labored under oppression—both waiting for the birthing pangs of God's promise to begin. Their continued fervent prayers of despair rang out in the heavens, birthing the Hebrew people into a new nation free from slavery and the birth of Samuel brought him out to be the prophet of the Lord.

Hannah's cries were not wasted and neither are yours. I don't know what your waiting season looks like. I don't know if it will be six months, a decade, or a lifetime but I do know that God sees you in your cries of despair. He knows what you beg for night after night. And just as those fervent prayers reached the ears of heaven, yours do as well.

In seasons of spiritual barrenness—when vision fades, prayers seem to echo back in silence, or the soul feels weary and still—God is not absent. He is forming a new vision within you, one that will be birthed through your waiting.

* * *

Lord, let Your Spirit reach every person reading this page. If there is anyone who has been crying out in despair or longing, I ask that You would meet them in their grief. I pray You would show them Your love and encourage them to seek You more. I pray for healing and fruitfulness — in bodies, in hearts, and in lives. I pray for stress and anxiety to fall at the feet of Jesus. Speak into the places of dryness in our lives: our spirits, emotions, relationships, jobs, any place needing Your presence. Lord, bring forth new life where there has been barrenness, just as You birthed a people out of slavery and gave Hannah her son. We cry out to You and worship Your name whether it be in fullness or emptiness. We love You. We trust that You hear us, just as You heard Hannah, just as You heard Your people in Egypt.

In Jesus' name,

Amen

* * *

Discussion Questions

- How do you think it felt for the people of Israel and for Hannah in their moments of grief and waiting?
- Have you ever experienced a season of desperation or grief? What did that time reveal about your relationship with God?
- Are there areas in your life where you feel empty or barren? How might God want to fill those places with new life or vision today?

Chapter 8

Ask, Seek, Knock

*"Pray as though everything depended on God. Work as
though everything depended on you."*
-Augustine of Hippo

I live in Southern California, in the vast 47,000-square-
mile stretch known as the Mojave desert. This desert spans
parts of California, Nevada, and Utah[44]. It's dry and hot—
rocky mountains, thorny shrubs, and basins cut by the rare
downpour washing down into the valleys. This is the barren
landscape where my husband and I decided to train for a fifty-
mile hike we planned to do later that year.

Everything I need is in my backpack. A tent, food, water. But
that "everything" weighs fifty pounds. It makes every step
heavier, slower, and it turns out that it's not everything I need.
The second day in we realize that our water is running lower than

---

44 Phillips, Cindy. "Mojave Desert Map, National Preserve & Ecosystem."
   Study.com, 2022, study.com/academy/lesson/mojave-desert-location-ove
   rview.html.

is safe. Water isn't just a comfort in the desert, it's a necessity. Luckily, there was a water tank installed for hikers of the Pacific Crest Trail in this region. So that night we loaded up on the water, as much as we could and tucked in for the night.

I wake to footsteps in the dark—shuffling, low voices. I check the time—3 am. I drift again and wake to more footsteps—4 am. What are they doing so early? My husband and I make a slow start at 6 am. The sun has already risen when we head out.

I realize our mistake the moment we start trekking up the rocky mountainside with direct sun. The climb up the mountainside was slow and punishing. There were no trees, no visible shade. At times, dizziness threatened to stop me from continuing. I pressed my face beneath the scratchy branches of the desert bush—just enough shade for some relief from the inescapable heat. A small mercy. I sighed in relief as we reached an altitude where trees began to appear. Finally.

I remember this hike being the one that truly prepared me for the 50 miles we later did between Mammoth and Yosemite. Nothing taught me to push through like that harsh experience in the desert.

This is the thing about backpacking—it's all in the steps. The lesson I learned is the only thing that matters in those moments of extreme difficulty is one step in front of the other. Persistence isn't measured in miles—it's measured in steps. One more step. Can I do ten more steps? I would count them—one, two, three... Can I do twenty-five? or one hundred more steps? Those steps were the only thing that got me to the finish line. The desert doesn't just test my legs—it tests my trust.

Not every season of waiting is stillness. Some seasons call us to persist—to fight. Some are calling us to count the next ten steps and then the next ten after that.

The Bible contains the motif of the desert throughout its pages. It serves as a setting that propels God's story forward and also stands as a symbol for the kind of deserts we walk through. The desert asks God's people, "Will you trust Me through the wilderness? Will you persist?"

The people of Israel had to do that for forty years—take step after step—trusting God to provide and fighting their own self-reliance.

Sinai and Mojave are very similar with their hot, arid climates. I can almost picture God's people taking the next step just like I did. Their season of wilderness, however, did not last days but years and that level of perseverance looked much different. They had to rely on God to bring them through the desert.

This trust took the shape of a pillar of cloud by day and a pillar of fire by night[45]—moving when the cloud moved, staying when it stayed[46]. It looked like water coming from a rock[47]. It looked like manna from the sky[48]—just enough per day.

The people of Israel had to fight the elements of the desert, they had to persist for years, but most difficult of all they had to fight to have trust that God would bring them through. They had to fight their own spirits to be aligned with what God had for them.

A common image of the desert is shepherds and their herds of sheep wandering the mountains from Sinai in those 40 years to David 400 years later in the Judean hills outside Bethlehem. The place where the sheep roam is stark with tufts of grass,

---

[45] Exodus 13:21 CBS

[46] Numbers 9:17-19 CSB

[47] Exodus 17:1-7 and Numbers 20:2-13 CSB

[48] Exodus 16 CSB

not bright green pastures of America, but an unforgiving place. Without the guidance of a shepherd, the sheep would not last long. The shepherd leads them to find food, while protecting them from cliffs and wild animals, always making sure they get the sustenance they need to survive.

Psalm 23 gives us the most familiar picture of God as the shepherd of His people. With these images of desert in our minds, it begins to read less like poetry and more like survival language. It starts with,

> "The Lord is my shepherd;
>> I shall not want.
>> He makes me to lie down in green pastures;
>> He leads me beside the still waters[49]."

When the Lord is your shepherd you do not go hungry. Even though there appears to be very little, He will give you what you need to survive. In the desert, this is usually just enough. The green pastures here are those tufts of grass that when you look at it in the right lighting then they appear green. It's not luxury, it's just enough. But sheep only lie down when they are satisfied. They only relax when they are safe. He gave the Israelites enough and He will give you enough. The Psalm continues with,

> "He restores my soul;
>> He leads me in the paths of righteousness
>> For His name's sake[50]."

---

[49] Psalm 23:1–2 NKJV

[50] Psalm 23:3 NKJV

In the wilderness, there are literal narrow, winding paths called paths of righteousness. These are places worn over time that provide the sheep a place of sure footing in the midst of treacherous terrain. Amidst the danger around you, the Lord is there to guide you with one step at a time—not with a wide road but a place with just enough room for your feet. The Hebrew word for righteousness here is ṣeḏeq[51]. It means justice, moral rightness but it also means just making the right decision. So as you are walking through that rugged wilderness, God will be walking right with you to help you make the right decisions at each turn.

> *"Yea, though I walk through the valley of the shadow of death,*
> *I will fear no evil;*
> *For You are with me;*
> *Your rod and Your staff, they comfort me.[52]"*

A staff in the hand of a shepherd is not to abuse his sheep, not to punish, but to guide. It's there to keep you from going toward something dangerous. At times it's even to keep wild animals from attacking. The shepherd does not lead through punishment—he leads through his voice. Jesus continues the imagery of shepherds and sheep when he says,

> *"My sheep hear my voice, I know them, and they follow*

---

[51] "righteousness, n." The New Strong's Exhaustive Concordance of the Bible, Thomas Nelson, 2009, p. H6664.

[52] Psalm 23:4 NKJV

me[53]*.* ”

A shepherd can make a call from the back of the flock and the sheep hear his voice and obey the command. There can be several flocks mixed together, but once the shepherd calls, only his sheep come. They are his sheep and his sheep follow his voice.

In the desert of our lives, we can attune our ears to hear the voice of the Shepherd Jesus and follow where He leads, even when we can't see clearly ahead of us.

This image of the desert is an example of what was required for the people of Israel and now us. If we trust, if we continue to walk in his ways we will be safe and satisfied. But we must choose to listen, to step, to resist the urge to chart our own path—especially because oftentimes it leads us off a cliff.

And just as the wilderness teaches us to take one faithful step at a time, Abraham gives us another picture of faithful persistence—not in walking but in asking.

There was such great evil that rose up in the cities of Sodom and Gomorrah. Violence and injustice were commonplace alongside sexual immorality. One such example takes place in Genesis 19 when two men came to stay with Lot. When they heard, men from different parts of the city came to his door demanding to violate them. In the face of this overwhelming wickedness, Abraham didn't retreat in despair, he didn't go silent—he stepped forward into dialogue with God.

The Lord was hearing the cries of the oppressed coming from Sodom and said before Abraham that He would destroy the city for their evil deeds but this didn't sit well with Abraham so he

---

[53] John 10:27 CSB

asked God,

> *"Will you really sweep away the righteous with the wicked? What if there are fifty righteous people in the city? Will you really sweep it away instead of sparing the place for the sake of the fifty righteous people who are in it? You could not possibly do such a thing: to kill the righteous with the wicked, treating the righteous and the wicked alike. You could not possibly do that! Won't the Judge of the whole earth do what is just?*[54]*"*

God responds that he would not destroy the whole place if there was fifty righteous people in the city.

Abraham doubles down on his question. *What about forty-five righteous?*

God would not destroy the city on account of forty-five righteous.

Abraham continued, all the way down to ten. *If there are ten righteous, would he cease to destroy the city?* And God agreed to save the city if ten were found righteous.

Abraham asked in faith for God to spare the righteous. He went from fifty to forty-five to forty to thirty to twenty to ten. To us, it may seem like a lot of bold bargaining—but God welcomed it.

Abraham kept asking—not because God needed persuading, but because God invited him into intercession on behalf of others.

This is a part of walking in faith—Abraham believed that God was faithful and just to hear him after six times of asking. He also wants you to ask—to come before Him again and again in

---

[54] Genesis 18:23-25 CSB

intercession for others before the Father.

Jesus, also, teaches us to keep asking, seeking, and knocking. Faith isn't just asking once—it's diligence in prayer. Jesus teaches his disciples something more about not giving up in His parable of the persistent widow. In Luke 18:1-8 CSB the story is written like this:

> *"Now he told them a parable on the need for them to pray always and not give up. 'There was a judge in a certain town who didn't fear God or respect people. And a widow in that town kept coming to him, saying, 'Give me justice against my adversary.'*
>
> *'For a while he was unwilling, but later he said to himself, 'Even though I don't fear God or respect people, yet because this widow keeps pestering me, I will give her justice, so that she doesn't wear me out by her persistent coming.'*
>
> *Then the Lord said, 'Listen to what the unjust judge says. Will not God grant justice to his elect who cry out to him day and night? Will he delay helping them? I tell you that he will swiftly grant them justice. Nevertheless, when the Son of Man comes, will he find faith on earth?'"*

What amazes me about this widow is that she doesn't sit around, hoping someone will give her the justice she deserves. She doesn't meditate on justice. She doesn't complain to her friends or bemoan about the unjust judge. She went to his door over and over again. She knocked and knocked, asking for the justice she desires. If she knocked once, would the judge have fulfilled her request? It seems likely that he would not have.

Only by coming over and over did the widow get her justice.

But God is not unjust. He is nothing like the judge. He is fair and hears the cries of His children. How much more will He give you what you ask when you come before Him again and again?

Jesus tells this parable to teach persistence in prayer—especially on behalf of others. It's to teach the disciples to pray without ceasing, to persist on behalf of others. There are many of us who are waiting—standing in the gap for someone else. Maybe we are praying for our lost children, our addicted family, the slow death of a marriage, our evil boss, or even for the brokenness of our world—our nation.

This parable stands as a lesson for us. That we stand and fight—we petition the Lord in prayer. The salvation of our children on our lips. The freedom for our family filling the air in our prayer closet. The restoration of relationship with our spouse. The repentance of our boss for all he has done. The return of our nation to the Lord! All of these prayers flowing up to heaven as a sweet incense.

The Lord doesn't need for you to knock over and over—you need it. Just as the desert strengthens faith, persistent asking shapes us. It refines you into the kind of follower that does not give up, that will fight for the lives and souls of the people around you who desperately need help.

The need for persistence does not mean your prayers aren't bold enough or aren't filled with enough faith. There are times in our spiritual dryness when it may take more time than we would like. These lonely wild places are moments where pressing into solitude, silence, and connection with God will develop you into a stronger follower. These moments are not acts of punishment from God, they are there to teach us, form us, and guide us into someone new.

Seek and you will find! Knock and the door will be opened

for you! Ask and you will receive! Step, step, step and you will make it through this desert of waiting and maybe you'll come out with the answer to your petition. And so waiting is never wasted. In the wilderness, God trains our feet. In prayer, He trains our hearts.

***

Lord, I pray that you would create in your people a persistence to fight for the salvation and restoration of this world. Just as Abraham asks for mercy for the righteous and the widow knocks repeatedly asking for the justice she seeks, let us be people that would knock repeatedly for those who need us. Lord, use these moments of waiting to teach us trust in the deserts and faithfulness to fight when we are called to fight. Help us to shift our question from "Jesus, why are you doing this?" to "Jesus, what are you up to in this? What are you teaching me?"

In Jesus' name,
Amen.

***

Discussion Questions

- What were some moments in your life where you could only focus on taking one step at a time—physically, spiritually, or mentally? How did you make it through?
- Why are there moments that call for you to fight rather than sitting in stillness?
- Who do you need to pray for like the widow knocking at the judge's door?

Chapter 9

It's a Party

"[There is] a time to weep and a time to laugh; a time to mourn and a time to dance[55]."

The dread pools in the bottom of your stomach. You thought you and all your people had made it. You look around briefly, seeing the same look mirrored on the faces of those around you. A scream echoes against the rock formations, bounces off the dark shadowy walls and back toward you. It ignites something in the throng. Many more screams resound in your eardrums. The bodies start to move around you—but there is nowhere to go.

The sea is before you and Pharaoh is behind you. Manic energy scores through your body as you realize you're trapped. As good as dead—or doomed to be returned to slavery.

You take one long breath and it centers you long enough to see Moses. He stands in the water, staff in the air as the sun sets before you. The staff hovers there for a moment and then

---

55 Ecclesiastes 3:4 CSB

plunges into the water.

Without hesitation, the water springs up as if called to attention by the staff. The water is pushed by an invisible hand. They separate until there is a path carved between the walls of water.

You do a double take—it's a path! There is a moment of fear. It's like jumping into darkness. It expands in your chest. Thoughts of drowning and death fill you. But what choice do we have?

So instead of waiting for the death you know is behind, you turn to the mystery that is before and walk. It is already dark, but as a collective we move.

It is morning as each of us collapses from exhaustion on the other side of the sea. The adrenaline is finally wearing off, leaving you empty. But you aren't safe yet. Pharaoh gives the command to advance and the peril has returned.

Before you allow terror to fill you, the water does something strange. It starts to churn and then it slides down in waves upon Pharaoh—water returning to its rightful place. A loud boom erupts when the last of the water slams into place. There is a beat of silence. Awe at what just happened.

In the face of that type of power, you know what it is you must do. You are Miriam, sister of Aaron, so you grab the tambourine in your hand. You shake it—slowly at first. Then faster and faster, hitting it against your palm. You start to move your legs. Tapping to the beat. Twirl. Sway. Move.

The women around you join, pouring all of the awe into this act of worship.

We survived. Our God, Yahweh, rescued us from our oppression.

Miriam and the women of Israel knew what time it was. It was the time to sing, dance, party—celebrate the miracle[56].

You might be asking yourself: What does celebration actually do for people who are still waiting and don't yet see deliverance?

Throughout the Bible God reminds His people that there is a season for everything. There may be a time to work but there is also a time to rest. There may be a time to be serious and focused but there is also a time to be happy, to party, to celebrate.

In Exodus 19:6 God names the people of Israel as a *kingdom of priests.* This was a concept that the people were not familiar with. They had seen a kingdom that had priests—Egypt—but they had no context to understand what it would be like for them to be a part of the priesthood as a whole people group. In the books of Exodus and then Leviticus, God was walking with His people, teaching them what it means to be holy, set apart—priests.

Most associate what God was teaching His people with laws and rules—not parties. But this is where the Festivals of the Lord are outlined. God orders His people to party. God wasn't just commanding rituals—He was commanding rhythm. Rest. Joy. Remembering through celebration. His people had to learn to trust the story that God was creating through them. While true in part, the whole story is not just about obedience; fundamentally, God's people were to celebrate to remind them the story is of God's goodness, His faithfulness, His love, and His mercy.

The people were to observe the Sabbath where they would do no work—reminding them that it's not what they do that makes them valuable but who they are as children of God.

The people were to celebrate Passover, remembering how God brought them out of slavery, followed by the Feast of Unleavened Bread commemorating the hasty escape from Egypt where there

---

[56] Inspired by Exodus 15.

was no time for the bread to rise.

There was the Feast of First Fruits celebrating the first harvest—being reminded to trust in God's provision.

Then the Feast of Weeks (Shavuot), which later also became Pentecost, marks the end of the harvest and remembers the giving of the Torah at Mount Sinai.

And the Feast of Trumpets (Rosh Hashanah), celebrating the start of the new year.

The Day of Atonement (Yom Kippur), a day for fasting, prayer, and repentance—being reconciled to God because of the sins committed.

Finally, the Feast of Tabernacles (Sukkot) reminds the people of the 40 years wandering in the desert and celebration of the harvest received that year[57].

Later the holidays of Hanukkah and Purim were also added as celebrations. Hanukkah rejoicing over the rededication of the temple and the miracle of oil lasting eight days when it should have lasted one. And Purim, remembering the salvation from Haman as described in the Book of Esther. And even with all these commanded celebrations, life was still hard.

God mandated that the people observe these festivals. A party was a requirement. Why?

These parties served as a way to remember and worship what God had done. It also brought the people of God together, served to build community. Each time the people partied—they became closer to God and closer to people. This is like the moment when an expert in the Law asked Jesus which was the greatest

---

[57] "Biblical Festivals: Does God Want Us to Celebrate Them? Why?" *Life, Hope & Truth*, 2025, lifehopeandtruth.com/life/plan-of-salvation/biblical-festiv als/. Accessed 9 Nov. 2025.

commandment. He said,

> *"'Love the Lord your God with all your heart and with all your soul and with all your mind.' This is the first and greatest commandment. And the second is like it: 'Love your neighbor as yourself.' All the Law and the Prophets hang on these two commandments[58]."*

As the festivals of the Lord were a reminder to the people about the faithfulness of God and the community of people, so too can the parties we observe. As we take a Sabbath, days of rest, observe Pentecost, Easter, Christmas, and all the other celebrations we create it can serve as a beacon of faith. God is doing amazing things in and through our lives as we wait. He has created the Body of Christ—the Church—for us to find a community of believers to worship and follow our God in unity. Our parties can remind us of that!

So take the palm branches and wave them, sing Hosanna on Easter for the risen King, read the story of the birth of Jesus on Christmas. Gather and take the Lord's Supper. Get baptized. Sing in worship at the top of your lungs.

But it isn't just religious celebrations but also everyday moments. For every birthday it reminds us of the value of every human life. For every wedding, we are gathered to rejoice and witness to the union between a man and his wife. For every retirement party we celebrate the years of hard work someone put into their lives. Baby showers. Gender reveals. Housewarming parties. Every time we make our own parties where we join together at a table with candles all around—

---

[58] Matthew 22:37–40 CSB

eat, talk, laugh—we are celebrating the Lord's breath in our lungs, the community he provided, the suffering he delivered us from. It's all His and it lets us find deep joy in knowing that He's present and partying with us. This isn't the kind of party that dulls our hearts—it's the kind that wakes them up to His goodness.

There are times when the party feels far away from us. We wonder how we can rejoice or celebrate when our miracle hasn't happened yet. What if we feel grief deep down in our bones? What if it simply hurts to live in our lives at the present moment? How can we party then?

It is those moments where it isn't just about the celebration but about the act of putting our trust in God—that he will eventually give us a reason to party but until then we will believe for the miracle even before we see it. Like Miriam and the people of Israel, they saw the incredible miracle of the parting of the Red Sea but they had just run from the only home they had ever known! They may have ended their season in Egypt but they were just beginning the season in the wilderness. But they still sang, still danced, still celebrated because if God could do one miracle, He could and would do another and then another. We can join into the community and be thankful for what we do have and believe for what we don't.

So sing like Miriam, dance like David, feast like Israel, and party like Jesus. Even when it feels like the Egyptians are right on your heels, the God who parts seas and fills cups still delights in the joy of His people.

* * *

Lord, let us take joy in this life that you have given us. Let us rejoice over your goodness, mercy, and salvation. Help us to find moments to set aside to celebrate all that you have done and all that you are going to do. When we are waiting, give us reason to dance, sing, and party. God, we trust you enough to celebrate before the miracle even happens.

In Jesus' Name,

Amen.

* * *

Discussion Questions

- What are some of your favorite celebrations? Why?
- How does this command to celebrate change the way you view the character of God?
- How can you add celebrations and joy into your daily life?

Chapter 10

Waiting with Proficiency

My parents are in a season of transition. They are coming to the point of retirement but, as is true for many in ministry, they are also open to the next assignment. The next thing is looming ahead but isn't here yet. A question rang out in the waiting. You may find it to be similar to yours. My mother asked, "But what do I *do*?"

She meant, do I continue to do what I'm doing? Do I continue to do the same thing until the waiting is over? Do I try to do the next thing? What is the work of my hands?

I think this is the heart of many of us who are walking through a transition that hasn't fully occurred yet.

I have seen many seasons in my life where what I had trained to do, the skills I acquired, were not being put to use. They lay dormant—waiting to be used in the right timing. My bachelor's degree, for instance, is in Film and Television. I trained for four years to be a film editor but once I graduated the Lord lead me in a different direction. Was the four years a waste?

No. It's never a waste. There were key moments where having those skills and abilities—the time that I spent—became of use when I least expected it.

There was a time I worked as an assistant to a pastor. I truly loved the work of ministry and so I went to get my Master's Degree in Theology and Ministry. Before I even finished, God lead me to be a middle school language arts teacher. So I had a Master's but I was doing something totally different from what I had been trained. Was it a waste?

Absolutely not. There would be no way I could be writing today if not for that time—and the waiting that followed.

Or take my current season. I've been serving and leading in worship for many years but today I find my passion on hold. I'm waiting to see when the Lord will next use me. Do I just sit here and wait for that next time?

The answer is no. So as my mother asked, "What do I *do*?"

I believe what the Lord would speak over you, me, and my mother today is to build proficiency in the waiting. Hone your skills. Develop your craft. In my case: sing, practice, worship in my living room, and find others to coach me as I wait.

The story of Joseph stands as an example of someone who did a lot of waiting but developed his gifts for the time in which they were needed.

Pharaoh continued to have dreams—night after night—that kept him awake. He couldn't understand what they meant but they returned. He called in all the advisors, magicians, and wise men he could find to interpret the dream but no one could do it. They weighed upon him and his heart felt heavy. He was becoming desperate when his chief cup bearer remembered someone—Joseph. He had interpreted dreams for the cup bearer and the baker while they were in prison.

So Joseph was brought immediately out of his place in the prison cell and was placed before Pharaoh's throne. There he was told the dream: Pharaoh dreamed of seven healthy cows and seven sickly ones, of full heads of grain and withered ones. The thin devoured the full[59].

This dream troubled Pharaoh. He felt the weight of it on his shoulders as the leader over the land. So Joseph interpreted the dream, as given to him by God.

> *"God has shown Pharaoh what he is about to do. Seven years of great abundance are coming throughout the land of Egypt. After them, seven years of famine will take place, and all the abundance in the land of Egypt will be forgotten. The famine will devastate the land. The abundance in the land will not be remembered because of the famine that follows it, for the famine will be very severe. Since the dream was given twice to Pharaoh, it means that the matter has been determined by God, and he will carry it out soon[60]."*

God had given these dreams to Pharaoh as a warning of what was about to come. Joseph had been given the gift to be able to interpret dreams. The Holy Spirit worked through him building this gift of interpretation all throughout his life.

Not only does Joseph interpret the dreams but he then provides Pharaoh with the wisdom of how to handle the dreams when he says:

> *"So now, let Pharaoh look for a discerning and wise man and set him over the land of Egypt. Let Pharaoh do this: Let him appoint overseers over the land and*

---

59 Genesis 41:17-24 CSB

60 Genesis 41:28-32 CSB

take a fifth of the harvest of the land of Egypt during the seven years of abundance. Let them gather all the excess food during these good years that are coming. Under Pharaoh's authority, store the grain in the cities, so they may preserve it as food. The food will be a reserve for the land during the seven years of famine that will take place in the land of Egypt. Then the country will not be wiped out by the famine[61]."

Pharaoh hears the wisdom of Joseph and sees the work of God and appoints him as a ruler over all of Egypt, only second to Pharaoh himself. Joseph uses his gift of management to oversee all of the food that comes into the storehouses and how to distribute them.

These gifts of dream interpretation, wisdom, and management did not come out of nowhere. They were developed over Joseph's entire life—over years of waiting he honed his skills and developed his gifting.

They could be seen all the way back in his childhood, when he had dreams of his family's sheaves of grain bowing down to his sheave, indicating him reigning over his brothers, mother, and father.

While his immaturity overshadowed the event, he was still learning he had a gift and was beginning to develop it.

When Joseph was sold into slavery, he found himself in the house of Potiphar where he was made manager of the whole household. He was in charge of all the daily work. While he was held in slavery, in the waiting, God placed him where his ability to manage would be developed.

---

[61] Genesis 41:33-36 CSB

After being falsely accused of making advances toward Potiphar's wife, Joseph was sent into prison. He was seen kindly by the warden and was made to oversee all of the prisoners. He developed his gift—working even in the darkest of places. He had every right to allow himself to be swallowed in sorrow, but he didn't.

Then, as the final rising action, there are two men in the prison with dreams. One is the baker and the other is the cup bearer. They share the dreams with Joseph and he predicts that the baker will be hung to his death and the cup bearer would be returned to his position. Both of these came to pass, leading to the moment where he is called in to interpret the dream of Pharaoh.

The experiences of Joseph's life honed and developed his gifts of dream interpretation and management, preparing him for his future elevated position. None of the dreams or positions were a waste for Joseph. They qualified him to do the work given by Pharaoh.

The gift of wisdom that is presented in his understanding of the dreams, unfortunately, had to be developed over the darkest moments in his life. He had to learn wisdom when he gloated over his brothers about his dream to rule over them. He had to learn wisdom when Potiphar's wife falsely accused him. He had to learn wisdom when he interpreted a rather difficult dream to the baker. All of these moments when he was at his darkest— slavery, accusation, prison—he was learning wisdom.

Sometimes the Lord isn't just refining what we can *do* but who we're *becoming.* Waiting seasons sharpen our spiritual abilities—listening, trusting, surrendering—so that when the door opens, our hearts are ready just as Joseph had to become ready. We are called to steward and hone our gifts no matter our situation or circumstance of waiting—that in the waiting God may be preparing us for greater uses of these gifts. This is like what Jesus said in Luke 16:10 CSB,

> *"Whoever is faithful in very little is also faithful in much, and whoever is unrighteous in very little is also unrighteous in much."*

When we aren't chosen, He's teaching us humility and how to keep from comparing ourselves to others. When the waiting continues for too long, He's teaching us perseverance. When we can't see how something will work out, He's teaching us trust. Everything we go through can be used by God to develop our character.

While not perfect, Joseph is an example for us of someone who did a lot of waiting and during those times of waiting he was able to develop the abilities and talents to be able to rule the kingdom of Egypt in the perfect time to protect his family and ultimately the people of God. God did not necessarily cause Joseph's suffering but he certainly used it. In Genesis 50:20 CSB Joseph tells this to his brothers,

> *"You planned evil against me; God planned it for good to bring about the present result—the survival of many people."*

It may seem like you'll never be able to use your talent again or you're not sure what to do with it while you're waiting but you have to trust that God has a plan for your gifts and talents. David, before he became King, spent years with the sheep carrying a sling and a harp unknowingly preparing himself for the throne. Even Jesus Himself spent thirty years in quiet preparation before

His three years of ministry. Hidden years are not wasted years—they're a bridge for becoming who we must be to carry what's next. God will exalt you, give you that position, allow you to use that gift in His timing. So to answer my mother's question, and yours—the waiting is for becoming who God has called us to be. Building proficiency in the seasons of in-between.

* * *

Lord, we give all our skills, gifts, and talents to You. We ask that You would give us opportunities to use them for the glory of Your Kingdom. Give us the patience to wait for your timing and give us the perseverance to continue to hone our skills until the time You have for us.

In Jesus' Name,
Amen.

* * *

Discussion Questions

- Have you ever asked yourself, "What do I do?", during your season of waiting? What has God spoken to you when you ask?
- What are some practical skills you could be developing in your moments of waiting?
- Has there been a time when you were able use your skills, talents, and gifts for His Kingdom?

Chapter 11

The Unnecessary Waiting

The dark heavy clouds drift over the sky as you make your way back home from your friend's house. They had talked you into watching a scary movie with them. Normally you don't do that because you know how easily you freak out. But you gave in.

You pray that the rain would hold back until you could pull into your driveway. Your prayer was answered just as you pulled up; fat drops of rain began to beat on your windshield.

You make a break for it as fast as you can to your front door, managing to keep as dry as possible. Finally, inside your cozy house you grab a tea, a blanket, a book, and cuddle up on your couch.

You jump with a start when a boom erupts outside your house. Before you have time to worry about what caused the sound, a flash of light skitters by your window.

You feel on edge, having a hard time turning your attention back to your book. And that's when you hear a screeching sound outside. You hope that it stops, not knowing what it is. But the grating sound hits your ears again.

Sweat covers your hands as you rub them together. There

is a tightness in your stomach and your body begins to shiver. Within seconds, your brain is sprinting ahead of reality. You begin to imagine all sorts of horrible things happening. Is it a monster or a killer outside? It's probably not, but your fear wins out.

You give up trying to read and you retreat to your bedroom with the blanket over your head like you were when you were 5 years old waiting for your mom to come and comfort you. You ask yourself, *"Why did I watch that scary movie?"*

If you were to pause your fear for just a few minutes, you would have found a cat outside your house incredibly upset about the puddle she fell into. But you didn't check. Your fear wouldn't allow you to check. You hid instead—waiting in your bedroom for the sound to stop. Why does something so small feel so big? There is actually a reason your body reacts this way.

There are a couple things happening at once when you are afraid. The amygdala in your brain kicks into gear and releases stress hormones like cortisol and adrenaline[62]. Your body responds with sweat, discomfort in your stomach, shivers, and other symptoms. And then your body decides whether you are going to fight or flee.

While this is happening, your cerebral cortex, which is the part of your brain that controls reason and judgment, becomes impaired. This is why you couldn't use your reasoning enough to see that the sound was a cat and not some serial killer.

The same thing happens when the danger isn't real at all— just fear of the future. This is where unnecessary waiting is

---

[62] Northwestern Medicine. "The Truth behind Fear." *Northwestern Medicine,* Oct. 2020, www.nm.org/healthbeat/healthy-tips/emotional-health/5-thin gs-you-never-knew-about-fear.

born—the kind that has nothing to do with God's timing and everything to do with fear. You begin to imagine all of these horrible things that could happen if you tried to pursue your dreams. The reaction in your body overwhelms your ability to think rationally—to set plans forward. Your body doesn't know the difference between the cat, a catastrophe, and the imaginary things that haven't happened yet.

So you flee from all of the things you could do, all the things God has called you to do—constantly living in the "what if" and never in the reality.

You are entering a place called the unnecessary waiting. You say this is not a good time to buy a house. You say it's not a good time to have kids. You say it's not the right time to open your business. Or join the prayer ministry. Or begin to serve others in a food pantry. Or write that book. Or join a choir. Or go back to school. You're too busy or you don't know how to do it. And so you wait for a "better time", even though this has nothing to do with timing—you're paralyzed by your fear unable to step forward.

There are times where a whisper of doubt begins to creep into our minds, telling us that there is no way we will ever be good enough. Our chest tightens at even the thought of failure. It would just be safer to not try at all. We wouldn't want to let anyone down or let ourselves look like a fool. So we miss out on open doors and opportunities all in the false name of being more prepared, planning, and wisdom but really it's just that haunting question in our mind: "Am I good enough?"

There have been many times throughout my life when I have asked myself the same question. One such time was in my 20s when I knew I had a call in ministry but I didn't quite know if I could do it. And if I'm honest with myself there were times during that season when, from the outside, I looked like I was walking forward, but in reality I was self-sabotaging behind the scenes. The fear within me pushed me toward inappropriate relationships and alcohol—creating deep hypocrisy in my life. This was all born from fear. Fear that I would never be good enough so why try.

The bible talks about fear often in its pages. The phrase "fear not" or "do not be afraid" depending on the translation can be found about 70 times. If you include some variations on the phrase then you'll come closer to 100 times. This makes it a main theme. The Lord is consistently reminding His followers to trust in Him and to not be afraid.

One of the most famous mentions of this phrase is when the angel came before Mary. He said to her,

"Greetings, favored woman! The Lord is with you.[63]"

Her heart began to race. Her palms turn clammy. She was greatly troubled by this greeting—unsure of what it meant—the uncertainty filling her body. So the angel said to Mary,

"Do not be afraid, Mary, for you have found favor with God. Now listen: You will conceive and give birth to a son, and you will name him Jesus. He will be great and will be called the Son of the Most High, and the Lord God will give him the throne of his father David. He will reign over the house of Jacob forever, and his kingdom will have no end[64]."

------

[63] Luke 1:28 CSB

[64] Luke 1:30-33 CSB

I can imagine the thoughts in her mind. *"Me? I'm chosen for this? Are you sure? What if I fail?"*

The angel was instructing her to fear not. First, she was not to fear him. He came to her to deliver a message—to bring her news. But he was, also, saying to not fear what was to come. This news had the possibility to be terrifying. Mary could have endured discrimination or even death bearing a son out of wedlock.

Now, God has given each of us free will and I believe Mary was no different. That means she could have said no and God would have respected that decision. But the angel's command to "fear not" was also about not fearing the repercussions of saying *yes*—God would be with her and keep her out of danger.

With this choice to accept, her life would be turned inside out, transformed overnight. Imagine if she would have said no, all of the things that were to come would have to be different. The Son of the Most High would have to be born another way. That blessing would have left her and gone to someone else.

But she said yes, as God always knew she would, telling the angel,

> *"See, I am the Lord's servant. May it happen to me as you have said.*[65]*"*

Mary did not allow her fear to overshadow her decision. She could have allowed the fear of the unknown, the future, death or discrimination paralyze her decision but she did not. She had faith and what was spoken over her came to pass. Mary's courage wasn't an isolated moment; Scripture is full of people who had to choose faith over fear.

---

[65] Luke 1:38 CSB

The Apostle Paul spoke this to his disciple Timothy,

"For the Spirit God gave us does not make us timid, but gives us power, love and self-discipline.[66]*"*

As followers of Christ, we have been given the power of the Holy Spirit. We are not to fear what others fear. No persecution, threat of death, lack of resources, or failure will ever be able to stand in our way. If God gave you a passion to do something, then walk forward into that calling without fear or trepidation because He is with you and will guide you.

There are times where it takes discernment to truly know if what you are feeling is fear or sound judgment. Fear stands out. It is loud, urgent, catastrophic. In converse, wisdom is calm, patient, invitational. Fear isolates. Wisdom invites counsel. Fear keeps moving the goalpost. One of the clearest signs that something is fear and not wisdom is that fear demands inaction, while wisdom—even when it says 'wait'—still invites obedience in small, faithful steps.

If you find that you are called to step forward, do not allow yourself to enter a place of unnecessary waiting because of fear. This is the type of waiting that you, not God or anyone else, put yourself in. Step out of that waiting into the fullness of what He has for you. Just as Mary stepped into her glorious calling as the mother of Jesus and just as Timothy was called to be loyal to the gospel and not be frightened in any way by his opponents; so you too are called to do something today—not waiting for tomorrow. Don't let a harmless sound in the dark keep you from stepping into what God has already prepared for you.

---

[66] 2 Timothy 1:7 CSB

* * *

Lord, I ask that you would help us to see that there is nothing to fear when You are with us. Give us courage and faith to step into the things You have called us into. Don't let our fear of failure, overpower our will to follow You. Keep us out of the unnecessary times of waiting—and help us step forward in what You have for us.
In Jesus' Name,
Amen.

* * *

Discussion Questions

- What fear has kept you in unnecessary waiting? Is there something that you want to do but are afraid of doing?
- What have been moments in your life where fear of failure has shaped the actions that you took?
- What are ways you can overcome fear?

Chapter 12

Kingdom of God

The Kingdom of God is like many things, and Jesus spent much of His ministry describing what it's like. His central message—woven through His ministry, His teachings, parables, miracles, especially in the Sermon on the Mount—is all about what God's rule looks like and how it breaks into human lives. He trained His disciples to live in the Kingdom and to carry it to the ends of the earth. Jesus' death and resurrection revealed it through the defeat of sin and death.

The Kingdom of God is described like a mustard seed (*Matthew 13:31–32; Mark 4:30–32; Luke 13:18–19*), that it grows from the tiniest of seeds into the largest of trees—starting small but shooting up to be great. It's like leaven (*Matthew 13:33; Luke 13:20–21*), permeating the community and culture around it. Each image layers on top of the other: like hidden treasure (*Matthew 13:44*), when found, is worth surrendering everything else to have. Like the pearl of great price (*Matthew 13:45–46*)—the Kingdom is worth the ultimate value.

But the Kingdom also separates—the good from the bad fish (*Matthew 13:47–50*), the wheat from the tares (*Matthew 13:24–30, 36–43*), the sheep from the goats (*Matthew 25:31–46*)—teaching us justice and final accountability.

It calls for a response—rewarding those who are faithful with little and giving them more *(Matthew 25:14–30; Luke 19:11–27)*, building one's life on Jesus *(Matthew 7:24–27; Luke 6:46–49)*, and inviting the poor, the lame, and the blind *(Luke 14:12–24)*.

The Kingdom reveals the heart of the Father through mercy, forgiveness, and transformation *(Matthew 18:21–35)*. It teaches those who have been forgiven to forgive *(Matthew 6:12, 14–15; Luke 7:41–43)*. It invites all into the grace of God—even if that acceptance comes at the very last minute *(Matthew 20:1–16)*.

It is leaving the ninety-nine to find the one *(Matthew 18:12–14; Luke 15:3–7)*. It rejoices when lost coins are found *(Luke 15:8–10)*. It shows how the Father lavishes great mercy on the one who was lost and then became found *(Luke 15:11–32)*.

It's within us *(Luke 17:20–21)*. It has come near *(Mark 1:15)*, but it's also not here yet *(Matthew 6:10; Luke 22:18)*. One must be born again to see it *(John 3:3–5)*. The poor in spirit are blessed with it *(Matthew 5:3)*. Those who seek it will find it *(Matthew 6:33; 7:7–8)*, and the one who enters it has faith like a child *(Matthew 18:3–4; Mark 10:14–15)*. Upon finding it, you must wait upon it, and in the waiting you discover it is worth the wait *(Luke 12:35–40; Hebrews 10:36–37; Romans 8:18–25)*.

But you have to be ready while you wait, at least, that was what the ten bridesmaids learned. Jesus didn't define the Kingdom with doctrine alone but through living pictures called parables that invite us to imagine what life under His rule looks like. This parable[67] starts like many others, "At that time the Kingdom of Heaven will be like…"

The bridesmaids waited for the groom to bring him into the

---

[67] Matthew 25:1-4 CSB

wedding ceremony. Five of the bridesmaids did not bring oil for their lamps and five did. Time passed slowly while they waited.

"He must be delayed," they surmised amongst themselves. Minutes became hours as their heads drooped and their lamps grow dim.

And then the stillness of the air broke with footsteps and shouts, "He's almost here!" The excitement for the groom was growing—they chattered lively. They all looked down to start to trim their lamps.

In horror, the five who did not bring any oil realized their lamps were going dim.

They begged their fellow bridesmaids, "please give us some of your oil! Our lamps are going out."

The five wise bridesmaids declined, "we don't have enough for ourselves and you. Go buy some for yourselves."

So they went searching for oil to light their lamps but while they were gone the groom arrived, went into the party, and shut the door behind him.

They pounded at the door, desperate to be let in. But the groom called out, "I do not know you." And they were shut out.

This parable mirrors a common cultural practice. When the bride and groom were engaged, the groom returned home to build a place for them to live—to make it ready for their lives together. The time this would have taken varied but eventually the groom would arrive to get married to his bride. But this could have been anytime of day or night so they needed to be ready to receive him. In this parable, some of the bridesmaids were not ready and so were left out.

This is not the first time that the Bible has used marriage language to describe the relationship between God and His people. In Exodus 19, God leads His people to a place under the face of the mountain. There He speaks to Moses and commands him to tell the Israelites,

> *"You have seen what I did to the Egyptians and how I carried you on eagles' wings and brought you to myself. Now if you will carefully listen to me and keep my covenant, you will be my own possession out of all the peoples, although the whole earth is mine, and you will be my kingdom of priests and my holy nation.[68]"*

God calls them His "own possession". He says they are His "kingdom of priests" and His "holy nation". In other translations it says "my treasured possession." He brings them under the mountain—a place that resembles the Chuppah[69], a tent under which Jewish weddings take place. The mountain provides a place of shelter and protection where God can put the marriage contract together. This is when each of the Ten Commandments and other laws were put together and presented to the people. Each of these commands serve as vows of commitment. The people's part of this covenant is to be faithful to God and "have not other gods besides me[70]", to make their relationship with Him first, and to keep from speaking poorly of their "husband". These commandments and rules mirror what a marriage contract might look like.

The people agree to the terms of the contract. So God and Moses go away to the mountain again, this is like the time the

---

[68] Exodus 19:4-6 CSB

[69] Solomon, Marty. "Under the Chuppah." *Blogspot.com*, 2021, makingtalmidi m.blogspot.com/2013/10/under-chuppah.html.

[70] Exodus 20:3 CSB

groom takes to make his home ready for his bride. While the "groom" is away the "bride" is preparing herself for his arrival. In Exodus 19, God tells the people, through Moses, to consecrate themselves and wash their clothes preparing themselves. Just like a bride would get ready for her wedding, the people of God were to get themselves ready.

But their faithfulness didn't last long. With a frightful turn of events, instead of preparing themselves, the people of Israel made a golden calf and began to worship it. In this grotesque image it would be like the groom returning from preparing a place for them to live, only to find his betrothed committing adultery. They had broken the contract before it was even official.

In almost any other situation, the contract would be void and the groom would have every reason to walk away, but here God does not leave. Even when the people can't keep their side of the covenant, He continues to remain faithful. This remains true today. We can't fulfill our end of the covenant. All of us sin and fall short of what is expected of us but God is still faithful. He was so faithful that He sent His only son to die on the cross so that both sides of the covenant are covered. Our part is covered by the blood of Christ and allows us to be His bride. In Revelation 19:7 CSB it says,

> *"Let us be glad, rejoice, and give him glory,*
> *because the marriage of the Lamb has come,*
> *and his bride has prepared herself."*

The parable of the ten bridesmaids represents the second-coming of Christ and His Kingdom. The five wise bridesmaids are those Christians who are ready while they are waiting. They are living out the Kingdom of God in the here and now. They are living their lives for Jesus while waiting in anticipation for His return. The oil in the lamps represents the believer's readiness. This calls to mind the Holy Spirit, who fills the believer with life and gives the power to continue waiting and working for Jesus. Finally, the groom is Jesus. He will be coming, we just don't know the day or the hour of His arrival.

This parable is not found in isolation. It is settled in a cluster of teaching from Jesus about the end times. Jesus uses a spiral teaching pattern here, employing several parables to explain and reexplain how we are to live in readiness and anticipation of the coming of the Kingdom of God in its fullness at Jesus' second coming. He layers image upon image—fig trees, days of Noah, servants at work, lamps burning, talents invested—all echoing the same refrain: 'no one knows the day or the hour,[71]' and therefore calling us to live in constant readiness.

Our lamps are still burning in the dark, and the night sometimes feels long. Yet the oil of the Spirit keeps us ready—faithful in the waiting, hopeful for His coming. While it's something we can't physically see with our eyes, it's something that should always be in our hearts and minds. While earthly seasons of waiting do not last forever, this kind of waiting endures until the day Christ returns. Every flicker of light in our lamps is a reminder of His Kingdom breaking through into the here and now.

* * *

Lord, help us to see how your Kingdom is present in our lives

---

[71] Matthew 24:36 CSB

everyday. Let us see your faithfulness, forgiveness, and dedication to your people and give us the ability to live out a response today. Show us how to wait in readiness for the Kingdom of God in the future. We praise You for all You've done.

In Jesus' Name,

Amen.

* * *

Discussion Questions

- What do you know about the Kingdom of God based on scriptures?
- Does the wedding imagery in Exodus change the way you see the ten commandments? If so, how?
- What are practical ways you can wait for the Kingdom of God with readiness?

Chapter 13

The Payoff

As a young adult, my family decided to visit Sequoia National Forest and find a hike there. We really did not plan ahead. In fact, we had a few water bottles with us—far from what we should have been carrying with us.

We found a map and decided upon a hike called the Marble Falls Trail. I really had no idea what I was getting myself into, but at the time I wasn't really in shape to hike long distances. Later, I found out that this was a 6.3-mile hike with 1,499 ft in elevation gain.

At the time, I found this brutal. Sweat poured down my face, a hitch in my side had developed from the climbing, and my feet were throbbing.

I will be honest and say, I contemplated quitting several times.

I looked over the steep drop-offs of the trail and couldn't remember why I agreed to this hike in the first place. After what felt like endless climbing, the trail finally began to level out. We turned a corner—and suddenly, there it was.

It was not what I expected—filled with awe, I took in the huge slabs of natural marble. Cool to the touch—I lay down flat listening to the water flowing around the rock. The white stone had swirls of grey and black, looking like a marbled cake.

It was marvelous, like nothing I had yet to see before. What turned this strenuous hike into a marvel was the payoff.

I now often seek out hikes like this, where I know there will be a gorgeous payoff at the end. All the work will be worth it because of the end. My favorites are still the ones I didn't see coming—the moments when I turned a corner and the beauty took my breath away.

A sense of overwhelm always fills my chest, chokes me up, and makes me pause in wonder—and I've forgotten all the hard work.

The payoff changes how you remember the pain. It's why we keep hiking. And it's also the reason that so many women have another child. If they remembered the pain of childbirth, they might never have another one. But that's not what they dwell on. They see that adorable, cooing baby in their arms and that pain that they endured fades into distant memory.

I can feel the truth of this myself in this moment. My 3-month-old is sleeping next to me as I write. Just moments ago he was smiling at me every time I turned in his direction but now he's nodded off. The joy of his chubby cheeks, soft skin, and his gentle snores almost make me want to do it again—almost.

Jesus talked about this kind of payoff with His disciples. He tells them that soon He will have to go away. He tells them that in a little while He will leave and in a little while He will return. The disciples were confused by His words. So He tells them,

> *"Truly I tell you, you will weep and mourn, but the world will rejoice. You will become sorrowful, but your sorrow will turn to joy. When a woman is in labor, she has pain because her time has come. But when she has given birth*

to a child, she no longer remembers the suffering because of the joy that a person has been born into the world. So you also have sorrow now. But I will see you again. Your hearts will rejoice, and no one will take away your joy from you[72]."

Jesus knows that upon His death, His followers will fall into a deep sorrow. There will be pain, discouragement, and mourning over the death of their teacher, friend, and who they believed to be the Messiah. There would be a void where Jesus had been.

But He tells them that this is not the end. There will be a time, very soon, that He will return to them. The time of sorrow will feel like nothing compared to the joy they will feel at His return. He is telling them the payoff at the end will be more than worth it.

This brings to mind, what I imagine we as believers will feel at the second coming of Christ. We currently live in a world filled with deep sorrow and suffering. There is war, genocide, anxiety, depression, sin, and sickness today but there will be a day when all of that has gone. That day sometime in the future is worth all of the suffering we endure today.

In Revelation 22:2 NIV it says,

"On each side of the river stood the tree of life, bearing twelve crops of fruit, yielding its fruit every month. And the leaves of the tree are for the healing of the nations."

This is a parallel image to that of the garden of Eden. Humanity's true place is in paradise, walking with the Lord in the cool of

---

[72] John 16:20-22 CSB

the day with access to all of plants and animals that live there. Here we could have lived in perfect unity with God and others—existing past the sin and death that have distorted and cursed our existence on this earth. But in this vision in Revelation, Jesus will renew the earth the way it was meant to be. In the future, we will be able to live our lives to the fullest possible measure—walking with God in a closeness we have never known, in a love that is currently unimaginable.

There will be a future where there is the river of living water, full of renewal, giving life wherever it goes. There will be a time when the people of Israel, as presented by the twelve fruits, will be restored to relationship with God. And there will be a healing of the nations where each and every one of us will find healing from our time on this broken earth.

And,

> *"He will wipe every tear from their eyes. There will be no more death or mourning or crying or pain, for the old order of things has passed away.*[73]*"*

This is the payoff of eternity.

Living on this earth means that our bodies decay. Death and sickness are part of the story of humanity but through Jesus we can find healing on this earth and in eternity. As in James 5:14-15 CSB let me ask,

> *"Is anyone among you sick? He should call for the elders of the church, and they are to pray over him, anointing him with oil in the name of the Lord. The prayer of faith*

---

[73] Revelation 21:4 NIV

will save the sick person, and the Lord will raise him up."

Whether healing comes in this life or ultimately in eternity, I am praying for you, believing that it's my job to pray and ask for your healing and God's job to do the rest. Just know that wherever you are, whatever sickness or pain is in your body, I am praying for your healing right now. In Jesus's name.

There is joy that walks with us before eternity. There are micro versions of the payoff we will see in the future. You will wait and endure, then see that beautiful vista, overwhelming waterfall, or huge slabs of marble and you will know you can make it through the difficulty until the next payoff.

Every season of waiting carries within it a pull, an ache in the middle where we haven't seen the end but we know there is a promise to come. Some of the payoffs we experience now on the earth, and others we will experience in eternity. But the sorrow is not the end, it's only the beginning.

* * *

Lord, help us to see our current suffering as temporary, that there will be a time where a new heaven and new earth are created and all of our mourning and pain will be something of the past. Show us the mini-payoffs throughout our lives, to help us to continue to step forward. I pray for healing for every sickness and broken body and believe for full restoration! I thank you for the ultimate payoff of eternity.

In Jesus' Name,
Amen.

* * *

Discussion Questions

- Have you ever experienced the kind of payoff in life, that fills you with wonder?
- How do you continue to hold onto hope even when you haven't seen the final result yet?
- Are there places in your life where you need healing?

Chapter 14

When He is Waiting on Us

My seasons of waiting feel like they are as numerous as the sand on a seashore. I wait for small things like my son to finally decide he's going to follow me through the mall instead of staring endlessly at a vending machine or for the light to turn green at the intersection or for Christmas to finally arrive. I waited for the larger things in life as well—for the right man to come along to be my husband, my baby to be born, the job I've been dreaming of. Life seems to be an endless stream of waiting.

There is a website[74] that counts the population of the world live. I watched the ticker for a minute, counting the amount of times it changed—up and down. It was about 100 times per minute. A person was born or died seemingly every second. When I closed the tab it was at 8,256,907,349 human beings on this planet. Now take that number and multiply it by the thousands and thousands of years we've been inhabiting the earth and then multiply that by how many mistakes we make per day and that number is the amount of times *God waits on us*.

---

[74] https://www.worldometers.info/world-population/

I can't imagine that type of patience. We make the same mistakes over and over, we ignore Him, we rebel, we become lazy or disbelieving and yet He still waits on us. He waits over each of our lifetimes for us to turn to Him—to seek Him. He waits because He is gracious. This is the wonder of His heart: He doesn't give up on us. Scripture describes it this way,

> *"Therefore the Lord is waiting to show you mercy,*
> *and is rising up to show you compassion,*
> *for the Lord is a just God.[75]"*

He wants to show you mercy. He wants to show you compassion. This is why Jesus hasn't returned yet to this earth. 2 Peter 3:9 CSB says this about the Lord's timing,

> *"The Lord does not delay his promise, as some understand*
> *delay, but is patient with you, not wanting any to perish*
> *but all to come to repentance."*

The Lord will keep His promises, He will return but His heart is to show mercy, to show compassion—so that many will come to repentance and accept Him.

This is all why timing is so important. We expect answers in our timing but we miss that His timing is aware. He knows what we need and when we need it. He knows when we sit down and when we stand up. He has searched our hearts and He knows us intimately.

In Ecclesiastes 3:11 NIV it states,

---

[75] Isaiah 30:18 CSB

"He has made everything beautiful in its time. He has also set eternity in the human heart; yet no one can fathom what God has done from beginning to end."

There is a perfect timing for each and every thing that happens in this life. We know that there is something beyond us but yet we are so focused on the seconds we live in the present that we often miss the big picture of eternity.

But God has eternity always in His mind. He knows who needs you to be ready to share the gospel—to be bold in encouraging those who don't know Him yet. And so He waits for you.

He knows you need time to learn how to be charitable and time to learn to live in justice toward your fellow man. Still, He waits.

He knows that you need to hone your skills and talents, to be proficient in the gifts He has given to you. And so He waits for you.

He knows what it will take for you to turn toward Him in prayer. His patience continues. And as He waits on us, He invites us to learn the rhythm of His mercy — to wait with Him, not apart from Him.

Waiting *with* God is different than waiting for Him. It's a partnership—a dance, where He knows the steps and He's ready to lead you. At first it may be difficult to find the rhythm but once you discover the steps and learn to follow then you'll be in tune. Waiting *with* God is less about the delay and more about coming into alignment with Him.

This type of waiting is not easy. Learning to wait *with* God also means learning to trust the process of His refining — the fire that shapes us into His likeness. It's like the process of refining gold or silver in a fire. Today, many refiners use chemicals to bring out the purity in these fine metals but in the time before modern science, fire was sometimes the sole process in taking out impurities. An Goldsmith or silversmith would place the metal into the hottest part of the fire. It's the place where other metals, the impurities, can be removed.

They would be patient, watching and waiting for the correct moment to remove the precious metal from the fire. The type of refinement the Lord provides is an act of love—the Refiner Himself never leaving the fire's side.

This process mirrors a prophecy written in Malachi 3. It begins by speaking of the messenger who will make the way for the Messenger of the Covenant. With the enlightenment of the New Testament, we understand the first messenger to be John the Baptist who makes the way for the Messenger of the Covenant, Jesus. And this Jesus will be a refiner to the house of Israel. Malachi says this,

> *"But who can endure the day of His coming?*
> *And who can stand when He appears?*
> *For He is like a refiner's fire*
> *And like launderers' soap.*
> *He will sit as a refiner and a purifier of silver;*
> *He will purify the sons of Levi,*
> *And purge them as gold and silver,*
> *That they may offer to the Lord*
> *An offering in righteousness*[76]*."*

He sits at the fire waiting for the perfect moment to remove the silver from the fire.

In the time of Malachi the people of Israel had returned from

---

[76] Malachi 3:2–3 NKJV

exile in Babylon—about 100 years prior[77]. When they had first returned from exile, there had been hope that once they rebuilt the temple, all the promises of the prophets before them would come true. The Messiah would come to unify the people of Israel and bring forth the Kingdom of God. But sadly that had not come to pass. These people proved to be as unfaithful to God as the ancestors before them that had been sent into exile in the first place.

That is where this prophecy comes in—Jesus would come to purify what had become unfaithful, to make their offerings righteous through His blood.

Ancient goldsmith or silversmith would sit at the fire waiting for the right moment. But how did they realize when it was ready? It has been told that they knew it was time when they could see the reflection of their face. Whether this is purely anecdotal or true fact is up for debate but either way it creates beautiful imagery.

Jesus would continue to refine the people of Israel until they looked like Him—He could see His own reflection through them.

This is the type of refining that we will go through as partners with Christ. There will be moments in our lives where it's so hot that we don't believe we will make it through—disappointment, pain, testing.

If God is the Refiner who never leaves the fire's side, then we are not passive metal waiting to be acted upon. We are invited into cooperation. Refinement is something God does, but it is also something we can resist—or receive. Instead of asking, "Why, God?" we can ask Him to reveal what we need to learn

---

[77] "Book of Malachi | Guide with Key Information and Resources." *BibleProject*, bibleproject.com/guides/book-of-malachi/.

in this season. We can attach ourselves to what God is doing by practicing spiritual disciplines—using prayer, solitude, silence, devotion as a way to stay near the fire instead of fleeing from it. Then we can ask God what impurities should be removed from our lives—and then actually respond in obedience.

There have been moments in my life where I have felt that refining. The process of walking through singleness in my twenties really pressed me. I felt alone, not worthy, insignificant. I tried to cover those feelings with something else but it never worked. Only when I recognized the season as one of God's refinement, did I find the blessing of that time of life and start to lean into the growth God was calling me to. God wanted to form and shape me in my singleness to help me see my beauty and worth even apart from a husband.

Maybe there have been moments you have felt a challenge like this. When we go through fires like these, the question becomes—when will it be time for us to be taken out of the furnace? Depending on the incredible plan God has for you and the particular season of refinement you find yourself in, the answer to this question will look different.

But I am confident of this: His refinement is not in vain. The more refined we become, the more we will reflect the Refiner, the more we look like Him.

This sort of change takes on another form in Jesus' analogy in John 15.

"I am the true vine, and My Father is the gardener. He cuts off every branch in Me that bears no fruit, while every branch that does bear fruit He prunes so that it will be even more fruitful. You are already clean because of the word I have spoken to you. Remain in Me, as I also remain

in you. No branch can bear fruit by itself; it must remain in the vine. Neither can you bear fruit unless you remain in Me."

Pruning is required to remove diseases, promote growth, and encourage fruitfulness in trees. The gardener cuts back the branches that need it. Just as God first prunes away those who do not bear fruit and also prunes us to cut away dead places so we can grow even more.

Pruning isn't enjoyable; it's cutting and chopping the sinful, broken, and self-serving pieces of us so that righteousness can grow in its place.

Jesus goes on to say that we must remain in Him in order to grow and bear fruit. Just like no branch can bear fruit by itself, we can't be righteous or holy without Him.

This type of partnership is what God is waiting on us for—to reflect the face of Jesus and to remain in the vine. When we look like Him and are connected to Him we can walk in a greater sense of fullness, following Him wherever He leads. In His mercy, He waits—not because He must, but because Love is patient enough to let us see His reflection.

* * *

Lord, thank you for waiting on us to become the partner you want us to be. Thank you for being patient even when we ignore or rebel against You. Refine us. Prune us. Make us into the type of follower who will cut away the dead and broken parts of us. We pray for your Kingdom to come but in Your timing.

In Jesus' name,

Amen.

* * *

Discussion Questions

- When have there been moments in your life where you were thankful for God's timing?
- Have there been moments in your life where difficulties turned out to be God refining you?
- What are practical ways you could keep yourself closer to the fire—allowing yourself to be refined or pruned by God?

Conclusion

"W ait...wait...wait...wait..." the monotone voice declared from the box attached to the light pole every time my 4-year-old niece pressed the button.

She was hopping from left to right, anxious to get to the other side of the street because that meant we were one step closer to her favorite place—Disneyland.

That monotone voice was an obnoxious reminder that she had to wait—just a little while longer before we got there.

There are so many different seasons of waiting and so many different ways we can respond to it. There is no one-size-fits-all when it comes to waiting. What may work for my situation in this moment may not work the same way again. What may work for you may not work for me. But somewhere in the middle of all these possibilities, there is always something God uses—something that strengthens, stretches, comforts, or transforms us.

At one time or another, we are all like my niece—waiting anxiously on our tippy toes for the moment the little green man appears so we can walk forward again. We all want to get to our destination. But truly it's not the destination that changes us—it's the time it takes to get there, the waiting we do in-between.

So, I hope this book gave you some encouragement during

your time in the waiting and I pray that God would change you more and more into the person He's called you to be. Just take a step forward—then another, and then another.

My hope is that these chapters have helped you see your waiting not as wasted time, but as sacred ground where God is moving.

As you move forward, I want to speak this blessing over you.

> *"The Lord bless you and keep you;*
> *The Lord make His face shine upon you,*
> *And be gracious to you;*
> *The Lord lift up His countenance upon you,*
> *And give you peace[78]."*

Amen.

And may you have joyful, wonder-filled travels on this journey of life.

---

[78] Numbers 6:24-26 NKJV

About the Author

Laura Paz is a wife, mom, teacher, and lifelong adventurer. She's married to her supportive husband, Victor, who can fix almost anything and keeps their family grounded. Together, they're raising three sons who fill their home with joy, noise, and endless stories.

She holds a Master's in Theology and Ministry and has spent her life serving in worship, missions, teaching, and church planting. Her heart beats for helping others discover God's presence in everyday life—waiting, wondering, and walking by faith.

Laura can often be found exploring new places, dreaming up adventures, or curating cozy reads through her mobile bookstore, *Adventurers, Darling! Books.* Her debut book, *Into the Waiting*, invites readers to find beauty in life's hardest waits.

You can connect with me on:

🌐 https://www.laurapazbooks.com

🔗 https://www.instagram.com/_adventurersdarling

www.ingramcontent.com/pod-product-compliance
Lightning Source LLC
Chambersburg PA
CBHW061237140726

47998CB00006B/2015